RESPONDER RESET

99 Real-Time Tactics for
Frontline Regulation

AK DOZANTI

Edited by Lil Barcaski

Cover Design: Kristina Conaster

Published by: GWN Publishing
www.GWNPublishing.com

ISBN: 978-1-965971-23-9

DISCLAIMER

This book is not a substitute for medical care, clinical treatment, or mental health services. The tactics described are short-term tools for stress and performance support, not solutions for long-term conditions or trauma.

Use your common sense. If you have a pre-existing health condition or injury that could be compromised by a tactic, skip it. Choose the options that fit your situation.

If you are experiencing ongoing distress or a crisis, call 911 or skip to the SOS section at the back of this book and scan the code for additional resources.

TABLE OF CONTENTS

SECTION 5: Emotionally Flooded 77

Read this when...

SECTION 6: The Job Bleeds into Your Life 89

Read this when...

DEDICATION

For every first responder and frontline warrior who's ever clenched the wheel, bit back the tears, swallowed the anger, or pushed through with nothing but grit when what you really needed was off-duty backup....

This book is for the moments you sat in the locker room holding it in, snapped in your own kitchen over nothing, or felt the lump in your throat mid-shift and tried your best to hide it. The times your humanness broke through the armor and you didn't know what to do with it.

My prayer is that these pages stand beside you in those moments, a steady hand, a reminder of your strength, and the truth that your humanness doesn't dull your "responderness", it sharpens it.

INTRODUCTION

This book pressed on me like unfinished business. Like it already existed and I just had to put it down on paper.

I saw it before I even started typing. Not on a nightstand. Not in a therapist's office. But in the glovebox of an ambulance. In the front pocket of a duty bag. On the kitchen table at the fire station. Beside the keyboard of a 911 dispatcher.

Tattered. Folded. Beat to hell from being used over and over, because the hands that reached for it needed something that could meet them where they were. No overthinking. No overexplaining. Just a tool to shift the weight when it starts getting loud.

That's what this is. Real-time support for high-functioning people in high-pressure environments. It's here for the moments in between, when you're still doing the job, still showing up but something is feeling off. When you don't need a breakdown or an entire breakthrough, you just need a damn reset.

On the surface, these might look like quick fixes. I need you to know *they're not*.

This isn't about suppressing what you're feeling so you can keep pretending everything's fine. You've already mastered that.

This is **micro-processing**, just enough movement to shift the tension, settle the system, and stop the spiral from picking up speed.

Each page is a pressure valve. A way to keep things from stacking so you can actually move the needle in the bigger picture.

To be clear: Regulation doesn't always mean "calm".

It means connection. It means you're not stuck in high gear or locked up with the parking brake on.

It means you're back in your body, aware, present, and able to move *through* what's happening instead of staying hijacked by it.

Harvard-trained neuroanatomist, Dr. Jill Bolte Taylor[1] found it takes just **90 seconds** for the chemical reaction of an emotion to metabolize through your body...*if you don't keep feeding it more story.*

That's what these pages are here for: to give you enough space to get through those 90 seconds without compounding the damage.

You need to know:

This book alone won't fix long-term chronic stress or deep-rooted burnout.

It's not a replacement for rest, recovery, therapy, or bigger systemic changes.

But it *will* help you in the moment, before you snap at the wrong person, shut down when you need to show up, or carry today's weight into tomorrow.

I wrote this guide because I've lived that edge. Worn the uniform. Carried the burden. Stood at the crossroads between "I've got this" and "I can't do this anymore."

This is everything I wish I had when I was trying to survive on grit, coffee, and pride.

If even one page helps you shift your energy, regulate your system, reconnect with your people, or stay grounded enough to come back tomorrow, then every word in here was worth it.

Let this book ride shotgun. Let it support you and guide you. Use it like the backup it was made to be.

Because you're not alone out there, and you were never meant to carry all of this without a way to *RESET*, *REFOCUS*, and *RISE*.

HOW TO USE THIS BOOK

DO NOT SKIP this, read this before you ever need the entries that follow.

This isn't a workbook. It's not a self-help experiment. It's a **field manual**, designed for real time use under real-life pressure.

You won't find long reflection prompts or theory in here. You'll find what works, when it counts.

This book was built for when you're on edge, but still holding the line. When you're showing up, but something underneath feels off. When your system's jammed, your patience is gone, and you don't have time for fluff.

RESET

Flip to the table of contents.

Every entry starts with *"Read this when..."* No guesswork. Just scan the list and find the one that fits your moment. Whether you're feeling flat, pissed off, checked out, wired, shut down, or unsure, **there's a page for that.**

That small decision to reach for something different, that's you interrupting the cycle. **Cracking this book open is the RESET.**

REFOCUS

Read the full entry. Don't skim. Don't cherry-pick.

You'll find:

READ THIS WHEN...

The trigger or pattern you'll recognize immediately.

BURNOUT BAIT:

The reflex or behavior that feels normal but keeps you stuck. This is the default burnout loves. DON'T TAKE THE BAIT!

TACTICAL TRADE-OFF:

The better move. Not deep work, a field-ready action that helps you interrupt the spiral. Quick. Low-profile. Something you can do in real life without drawing attention.

WHY THIS WORKS:

Short science-based explanation. No fluff or jargon. Because when you understand it, you're more likely to use it.

LOCK IT IN:

The wisdom you carry with you into the next call, the next conversation, the next version of you.

You'll see some of the tactics might feel unfamiliar at first, and that's on purpose.

They're drawn from proven methods grounded in neuroscience and somatic regulation, including things like bilateral stimulation, orienting responses, proprioceptive input, and EMDR-inspired movement.

These are body-based strategies designed to help you reset your system and regain control under pressure.

It might feel strange the first time you try one. *That's normal.*

Lean in anyway. The payoff is in the doing.

Keep a journal nearby, or write in the margins. Doesn't have to be deep, just enough to track what helped, what didn't, and what keeps showing up. Patterns matter. And noticing them is half the battle.

When you take the time to slow down, scan your system, do the damn trade-off, and **REFOCUS**.

RISE

This part is on you.

If you don't do it, it doesn't work. Period. Reading won't regulate your nervous system. Nodding along won't change anything.

This book can't do the work for you. But it can call your attention back to what matters before the damage spreads. **Action is the pattern interrupt. Ownership is the exit strategy.**

That moment you step back into your life a little more grounded, a little more aware, is your RISE.

MAKE IT PART OF YOUR GEAR

This isn't something you keep pristine on a shelf. It's something you keep **within reach**. Banged up. Dog-eared. At the ready.

Put it where you'll actually grab it:

- Glovebox
- Duty bag
- Locker
- Side pocket of your gear
- Bathroom counter at 2 a.m. when the day's still buzzing in your body
- On your nightstand when you're overthinking that call

Pages folded. Spine cracked. Corners worn. That's the goal. A tool doesn't work if it stays clean.

ABOUT THE PARTNER DEBRIEFS

The final section is built for **two people**. Not just you.

They're short, intentional tools to help process tension, heavy calls, or emotional residue **with someone else, before it calcifies.**

Use them:

- After a call with your crew
- Once you're home with your spouse
- During the in-between when neither of you want to talk, but you both feel it

This is not a substitute for a CISM peer team debrief. That has its place, and you know when it's needed. These are for the moments that don't get formal support, where most of the residue lives.

IN CASE OF A TRUE SOS

You'll find an **SOS QR code in the back** of this manual. (Underneath, you'll find space to write down numbers of local peer support contacts and team members you trust.)

If you're experiencing intense symptoms: suicidal thoughts, panic attacks, flashbacks, disconnection from reality, or a level of darkness you can't talk yourself out of, **scan the code.** It'll take you to a private, curated list of crisis resources. Not an ad. Not a rabbit hole. Just support that actually knows this world.

There's a time for tactical trade-offs.

And there's a time for strategic reinforcements.

Know the difference. And make the call.

BOTTOM LINE

This book isn't here to inspire you. It's here to **remind you what you're still capable of**, and help you act on it in real time.

We aren't made to carry this alone. Use the tools. Make the trade-off. Then get back in the fight... *clearer, calmer, and more in control.*

Because the job matters, but in case you forgot, YOU ARE THE MISSION. Protect accordingly.

Read this when you're
Wired

I once dropped an f-bomb over open radio waves. I was going hot to a fight call, keyed up, trying to clear an intersection, and some car blew through a red light like I wasn't even there. I hit the horn, yelled instinctively, and didn't realize I still had my thumb on the mic.

When I pulled up and stepped out, my coworker looked at me deadpan and said, "You mad, bro?"

I said no... cool as ever. Then he told me what went out over the air. And I realized I was so mad *I didn't even know I was mad.* That's how it works sometimes. You don't notice the tension until it leaks. You don't feel the pressure until it punches through your tone, your timing, and your reactions.

This section is full of quick, physical trade-offs to burn off what your body's still carrying. The clench in your jaw. The fists you didn't know were balled up. The edge you can't name but everyone else can feel. You don't need a fix; you need a release. Something that meets your system where it's at without making it a whole thing.

Start here. Move it through. Then see what's left.

1 | Read this when *your brain won't clock out*

BURNOUT BAIT:

Your default might be to scroll your phone, replay the whole shift, pour a drink, or lie in bed hoping your brain will shut up on its own. You're exhausted, but your system hasn't caught up.

TACTICAL TRADE-OFF:

5-MINUTE MANUAL RESET

Put your phone face-down like it just pissed you off. Set a 5-minute timer. Do something mindless and physical: fold laundry, wipe down your boots, reorganize gear, mess with a pen. Not to be productive but to give your hands a task while your brain takes a knee.

WHY THIS WORKS:

Simple, low-focus movements tell your brain to chill out. When your hands move, the system calms and the noise fades. Finishing the task closes the moment.[2]

LOCK IT IN:

Your brain thinks the shift isn't over. Show it different. Put your hands on something small, finish it, and prove to yourself you're off-duty now. *Peace doesn't wait for you... you create it.*

2 | Read this when *your body's buzzing but on empty*

BURNOUT BAIT:

Your default might be to crash on the couch but still feel wired. Scroll, snap at someone, or just sit there buzzing like a live wire with no outlet.

TACTICAL TRADE-OFF:

HEEL-DRIVE DUMP

Stand up. Plant your feet. Drive your heels into the ground for five seconds, like you're trying to snap a board under your boots. Then exhale hard like you're blowing out a fire. Repeat 2-3 rounds. It pushes the excess energy down and out without draining you.

WHY THIS WORKS:

Pushing through your heels tells your body you're grounded and stable. The hard exhale kicks in your calming system, literally. Studies show this combo boosts recovery and helps your system settle down.[3]

LOCK IT IN:

Buzzing with nowhere to go will chew holes in you. Drive it down through your heels, push it out with your breath, and stand steady. *Build the calm from the ground up.*

3 | Read this when *you're about to snap and don't know why*

BURNOUT BAIT:

Your default might be to lash out, slam something, stew in silence, or pick a fight over nothing. You're overloaded and your body's looking for a target.

TACTICAL TRADE-OFF:

WALL PRESS RESET

Find a wall. Press your palms into it like you're trying to shove the building over. Engage your whole body, core, legs, and jaw. Hold for 10 seconds. Exhale. Let go. Repeat 2–3 times. It's fight energy without the damage. You burn it off without blowing up.

WHY THIS WORKS:

Pressing hard gives your body the fight it's looking for without wreckage. The exhale shuts it down clean. This clears the adrenaline spike instead of stuffing it down.[4]

LOCK IT IN:

Pressure without a release point always finds one. Put it into the wall, the breath, the body, not the people around you. *Strength is directing force before it does the damage.*

4 | Read this when *you keep replaying that one call*

BURNOUT BAIT:

Your default might be to mentally rewatch it on loop, pick it apart, or try to shove it down and move on. But your brain keeps hitting play.

TACTICAL TRADE-OFF:

COUNTDOWN INTERRUPT

In your head, count backwards from 20 while slowly scanning the room RIGHT to LEFT. Then do it again. No phone, no fix, just shift your focus. It forces your brain into a new lane without needing to leave the room. That loop can't hold if your eyes and mind are on a different track.

WHY THIS WORKS:

Visual tracking tugs your attention away, calming the alarm system in your brain. Counting and scanning hijacks the loop, your brain can't replay and re-route at the same time.[5]

AFFIRM IT:

Your brain will loop it until you force a reset. Break the rhythm, redirect your focus, and take command of the moment. *The call is over, you're still here.*

5 | Read this when *you're too amped to sit still*

BURNOUT BAIT:

Your default might be to pace, snap at someone, overdo it at the gym, or scroll to distract yourself while your body buzzes like it's still mid-call.

TACTICAL TRADE-OFF:

STATIC SPRINT

Run in place, shadow box, or shake out your hands and feet, HARD, for 10 seconds. Then stop. Repeat once or twice. It's controlled chaos that clears adrenaline without needing space, gear, or a full workout. You're not training, you're discharging.

WHY THIS WORKS:

Short bursts of movement burn off the excess charge. Your body gets the memo that the threat has passed.[6]

LOCK IT IN:

Adrenaline has one job, to keep you moving. That doesn't mean you have to pace it out all night. Burn it quick, stop on purpose, and let your body know the fight is over. *Movement ends when you decide it ends.*

6 | Read this when *your jaw is tight and your fists are clenched*

BURNOUT BAIT:

Your default might be to grind through it... literally. Clenched teeth, tight fists, shoulders up to your ears. You're bracing like something's about to pop off.

TACTICAL TRADE-OFF:

JAW TAP + RELEASE

Lightly tap the hinge of your jaw with your fingertips. Open your mouth wide like a yawn. Exhale... loud and slow. Repeat 3x. It's a quick release to fight tension hiding in plain sight. Loosen the grip before it turns into a blow-up or a migraine.

WHY THIS WORKS:

Stress can hide in the jaw. Tapping and exhaling drops the fight before it takes over.[7]

LOCK IT IN:

Your body's bracing for impact that isn't coming. Loosen the jaw, open the hands, and stand steady on purpose. *Readiness without tension is real power.*

7 | Read this when *caffeine backfires*

BURNOUT BAIT:

Your default might be to grab another energy drink, even though your hands are already shaking and your thoughts are running laps. You're chasing focus, but getting static.

TACTICAL TRADE-OFF:

HYDRATE + HOLD

Chug 8 oz of cold water. Then press your palms together, HARD, for 10 seconds while breathing slow through your nose. Repeat. Water cools the internal system. The palm press gives your body pressure without more stimulation. It's a hard reset without the chemical spike.

WHY THIS WORKS:

Cold water cools your system fast and activates the vagus nerve. Pressing your palms together gives your body the grounding signal it's looking for.[8]

LOCK IT IN:

Your body's already red-lined, more fuel just keeps it stuck there. Cool it down, ground it, and take charge without the crutch. *Focus is built from regulation, not another hit.*

8 | Read this when *you're short-tempered with your crew or your family*

BURNOUT BAIT:

Your default might be to snap, shut down, or say something you don't mean, then stew in guilt after. You're overloaded, and it's leaking out sideways.

TACTICAL TRADE-OFF:

FIST-TO-OPEN DRILL

Squeeze your fists like you're wringing out a towel. Then open your fingers wide, like you're trying to stretch them off your hands. Repeat 5x. It clears the physical charge before it becomes a verbal one. A few rounds of this and the fuse resets.

WHY THIS WORKS:

Clench and release tells your system it's safe to drop the fight mode and shift into grounded control.[9]

LOCK IT IN:

The fuse is short, but it's still yours to control. Dump the charge before it leaks on the people who matter most. *Protecting them means regulating you.*

9 | **Read this when *you're hyped up but there's nothing to do***

BURNOUT BAIT:

Your default might be to fidget, overanalyze, pick a fight, or look for something, *anything*, to fix. Your body's charged, but there's nowhere for it to go.

TACTICAL TRADE-OFF:

SHOULDER SHOCK DROP

Lift your shoulders up slow like you're bracing. Hold for a beat. Then drop them fast with a sharp exhale, like you're shaking something off. Repeat a few times. It looks like a stretch, but your system knows it's a discharge.

WHY THIS WORKS:

Intentional tension + release signals completion to your nervous system. It's a fast way to burn off stored energy without spinning your wheels.[10]

LOCK IT IN:

Idle charge hunts for chaos. Drop the shoulders, breathe it out, and reset. *Energy isn't the enemy, misdirection is.*

10 | Read this when *you're yelling more than usual*

BURNOUT BAIT:

Your default might be to raise your voice before you even realize it, cutting people off, snapping mid-sentence, or overreacting to small stuff. The volume's not about them—it's about your system peaking.

TACTICAL TRADE-OFF:

BREATH-LEAD RESET

Before your next sentence, pause and breathe just long enough to feel your ribs move. Inhale slow, exhale slower. No one has to know. But your nervous system will. It's a quiet reset that buys you space to respond instead of react.

WHY THIS WORKS:

Slow breath means slower reactions. Your breath sets the pace before your mouth does.[11]

LOCK IT IN:

Volume doesn't equal strength. Command comes from calm. Lead with breath first, words second. *Control is what makes your voice carry weight.*

11 | Read this when *you're stuck on scene and can't regulate*

BURNOUT BAIT:

Your default might be to zone out, disconnect, or white-knuckle through it. You're there physically, but your system's either racing or frozen.

TACTICAL TRADE-OFF:

ANCHOR TOUCH

Place your palm flat on your sternum or vest. Breathe into the pressure, slow and steady. No one has to see it. No words required. Just presence. If it helps, repeat: "I am here now." It's a quiet override button your body understands.

WHY THIS WORKS:

Self-contact tells your body "You're here," and pulls you back into the moment.[12]

LOCK IT IN:

Your body wants to check out, but you don't have that luxury. Anchor in, hand to chest, breath steady, and call yourself back to now. *Presence is the sharpest tool you carry.*

12 | Read this when *your body says "fight" but your brain says "chill"*

BURNOUT BAIT:

Your default might be to white-knuckle it, snap at someone, or silently stew while pretending everything's fine. Your mind says let it go, but your body's still geared up to throw hands.

TACTICAL TRADE-OFF:

GLUTE CLAMP OVERRIDE

Squeeze your glutes and thighs like you're bracing for impact. Hold five seconds. Release. Repeat 3x. It redirects the fight charge without needing a target. Tension meets structure and your system gets the memo.

WHY THIS WORKS:

Big muscles burn fight energy fast. It's a safe outlet that tells your body to stand down.[13, 14]

LOCK IT IN:

Conflict between mind and body burns you from the inside out. Channel it into muscle, release it, and reset. *Discipline is giving your body orders it can follow.*

13 | **Read this when *everything feels urgent, but nothing actually is***

BURNOUT BAIT:

Your default might be to move faster. Check everything twice. Answer texts you don't need to. Feel like you're behind, even when nothing's waiting. It's your system talking, not the situation.

TACTICAL TRADE-OFF:

BILATERAL GROUND + CENTER

Plant both feet. Shift your weight onto your right foot. Look left. Name one thing you see. Shift your weight to your left foot. Look right. Name one thing you see. Repeat three rounds. You're syncing with the room, not the false alarm in your head.

WHY THIS WORKS:

Shifting your weight while scanning left and right gives bilateral input that calms the alarm system. Naming objects re-engages focus and locks you into the present.[15, 16]

LOCK IT IN:

False alarms will run you ragged if you let them. Slow down, ground down, and prove to yourself the world isn't on fire. *Constant urgency is a liar; clarity tells the truth.*

14 | Read this when *you're trying not to punch a wall*

BURNOUT BAIT:

Your default might be to slam a door, throw something, clench your fists, or feel that familiar heat rise in your chest. You're maxed out and your body wants a target.

TACTICAL TRADE-OFF:

KNUCKLE LOCK

Interlace your fingers tight. Press your thumbs into each other like you mean it. Hold. Breathe. Let the charge burn through your grip instead of your surroundings. It's pressure without destruction. A silent outlet for the noise.

WHY THIS WORKS:

Locking your hands gives the excess energy and tension somewhere to go that won't break skin, walls, or trust.[17]

LOCK IT IN:

Your fists aren't the enemy, but walls and people don't deserve the hit. Grip hard, lock in, and burn the charge through your hands. *Power means nothing if you can't control where it lands.*

15 | Read this when *you're pacing like a caged animal*

BURNOUT BAIT:

Your default might be to pace aimlessly, rant in your head, or wear a path in the floor. You're restless, trapped, and your system's circling something it can't solve.

TACTICAL TRADE-OFF:

BOX WALK DRILL

Walk in a square. One side = inhale. Next = hold. Third = exhale. Fourth = hold. Keep the pattern going as many laps as needed. It gives the movement structure and your breath a job. Controlled motion calms the chaos.

WHY THIS WORKS:

Breath plus steps gives your brain a pattern to follow. Chaos can't hold when motion has structure.[18]

LOCK IT IN:

Restlessness without direction is wasted fuel. Box it in, give it structure, and take command of the steps. *Controlled movement is controlled mind.*

Read this when you're
Numb or Shut Down

This isn't theory for me; this is MY default. My boogeyman.

When I was 17 my best friend died by suicide, I have zero recollection of the three months following her death. None. I worked two jobs. I went on family vacations. I smiled in pictures. And I have zero recollection of any of it. My brain did what it was wired to do: shut down, go cold, disconnect from everything that hurt. I got quiet. Robotic. Functional. But I wasn't there. I was checked out, just going through the motions.

That's what this section is about.

These are the moments when you're not falling apart, but you're not really present either. When you're sealed off so tightly you don't even realize it's happening. And eventually, what you thought you compartmentalized starts to leak out.

I wrote these pages because I know that freeze. I know what it costs when you live in that shut-down space for too long. And I know what it takes to start feeling again, without letting it drown you.

This isn't about snapping out of it. It's stepping back in, slow and steady, before the numbness eats more than it already has.

16 | **Read this when *you're stuck on autopilot***

BURNOUT BAIT:

Your default might be to keep pushing through on autopilot. Same steps. Same script. Same blank tone. You're technically functional, but totally checked out.

TACTICAL TRADE-OFF:

PATTERN DISRUPT

Interrupt the sequence. Change one thing. Move your watch to the other wrist. Swap pens. Use a different door. Change the radio station. Minor disruption, major reset.

WHY THIS WORKS:

Even tiny shifts in routine light up new neural pathways. That novelty pulls your brain out of autopilot and brings presence back online.[19]

LOCK IT IN:

Autopilot keeps you moving but steals your presence. Break the loop, shift one thing, and prove you're still in control. *Even the smallest change is evidence you're still here.*

17 | **Read this when** *you can't make yourself move*

BURNOUT BAIT:

You might freeze in place, physically unable to start. Staring at the wall. Gripped by stillness. The will to move feels gone. Even blinking feels like too much.

TACTICAL TRADE-OFF:

RHYTHM RESTART

Pick one rhythm, slow and steady to start:

- Tap your fingers on your leg.
- Bounce your heel in your boot.
- Lightly drum on the steering wheel.
- Keep it steady, 10 seconds minimum. Then breathe in through your nose, out through your mouth. Rhythm builds momentum. Breath carries it forward.

WHY THIS WORKS:

Steady rhythm helps restart movement. It gives your body a beat to follow and signals your brain that it's time to get going again.[20]

LOCK IT IN:

Freeze isn't forever. Start with rhythm, build with breath, and let motion carry you forward. *Momentum is built one beat at a time.*

18 | Read this when *you feel blank but keep going*

BURNOUT BAIT:

Your default might be to keep performing while feeling nothing. You show up, say the right things, do the job, but the emotion never kicks in. It's like watching your own life from behind glass.

TACTICAL TRADE-OFF:

PRESENCE RECALL RESET

- Tap your fingers gently against your chest or collarbone.
- While tapping, recall one moment when you felt fully alive, laughing with someone, crushing a task, watching a sunset.
- Hold the image. Let the memory land in your body, not just your mind.

WHY THIS WORKS:

Touching your body while remembering a real, positive moment helps connect emotion back to your system. It pulls the memory out of your head and into something you can actually feel.[21]

LOCK IT IN:

Flat moments don't mean you're finished. They're cues to re-engage. Tap in, remember something real, and let your system catch that spark again. *Aliveness answers when you call it forward.*

19 | Read this when *you zone out and can't snap back*

BURNOUT BAIT:

You catch yourself zoning out, eyes locked, brain offline. Time slips. You're not thinking, not feeling. Just frozen in that blank stare with no idea how long it's been.

TACTICAL TRADE-OFF:

BLINK + BILATERAL RESET

- Blink three times. Slowly move your eyes to the far left. Pause.
- Come back to center, blink three times again.
- Now shift your eyes to the far right. Pause.
- Repeat three rounds. You're reactivating focus without forcing it.

WHY THIS WORKS:

Blinking breaks visual freeze. Paired with side-to-side eye movement, it helps the brain reorient, re-focus, and exit shut-down mode gently and without overwhelm.[22]

LOCK IT IN:

Locking up doesn't serve you. Break it with movement, a blink, a shift, a scan, and put yourself back in command. *Focus returns the second you demand it.*

20 | Read this when *you feel disconnected from everyone*

BURNOUT BAIT:

You might default to isolation. Stay quiet. Keep your head down. Not because you don't care, but because connection feels too far away, too hard to start, or like nobody would get it anyway.

TACTICAL TRADE-OFF:

MICRO-CHECK PROTOCOL

Ask one person a basic question:

"You just get here?"

"Have you seen [insert name]?"

"Do you know if there's coffee?"

Doesn't matter what. It's not about depth. It's about contact. As you speak, roll your shoulders back, gently. That physical cue tells your body it's safe to engage again.

WHY THIS WORKS:

Small interactions plus open posture switches your body into social engagement mode. It gives your system a safe way to re-enter connection without pressure.[23]

LOCK IT IN:

Disconnection shrinks your world fast. Break the silence with a small signal... a nod, a word, a presence. *Connection grows the moment you choose to reach.*

21 | **Read this when** *everything feels heavy*

BURNOUT BAIT:

You might try to muscle through it. Shoulders tight. Holding it all in your body without even noticing. The weight isn't just emotional, it's physical. Like you're carrying the whole shift on your spine.

TACTICAL TRADE-OFF:

SURFACE SUPPORT RESET

Find a solid surface, wall, chair, locker. Sit or lean back until it takes your weight. Let your spine press into it. Exhale. Let the surface carry what your body can't.

WHY THIS WORKS:

Resting your back against something solid helps your nervous system recognize support, easing muscle tension and grounding your body. It signals, it's safe to let go.[24]

LOCK IT IN:

Weight doesn't mean carry it alone. Let the surface hold you, drop your spine into support, and release what isn't yours to grip. *Strength includes knowing when to lean.*

22 | **Read this when *it's hard to care, even though you know you should***

BURNOUT BAIT:

You're not heartless. You're just blocked. Between the noise, the stress, and everything unresolved, it's no wonder care can't break through. You're not broken; you're barricaded.

TACTICAL TRADE-OFF:

BARRIER SWIPE RESET

- Stand or sit. Extend your hands in front of you.
- Now swipe them outward like you're clearing smoke, cobwebs... or bullshit... out of your space.
- Do it slow and firm. Repeat 5x.

Clear what's in the way. Then re-ask: *What's still worth showing up for?*

WHY THIS WORKS:

Your brain links physical gestures with emotional states. Swiping your hands outward externalizes the overload and makes space for clarity to come through.[25]

LOCK IT IN:

Care gets buried, not erased. Clear the clutter, swipe out the noise, and give space for what still matters to surface. *What you value always fights its way back, clear the path.*

23 | Read this when *you can't explain what you're feeling*

BURNOUT BAIT:

Your default might be to brush it off, shut it down, or power through. You don't have the words, so you act like there's nothing there. But there is. It just doesn't make sense yet.

TACTICAL TRADE-OFF:

WALK IT OUT RESET

Stand up. Walk a hallway, a perimeter, or just from one end of the room to the other, slow and steady. Keep your eyes forward. No phone. No talking. Let the motion do the sorting. You're not avoiding. You're moving the static out of your head.

WHY THIS WORKS:

Steady walking activates both sides of the brain and organizes scattered thoughts. It helps your system process emotion without needing words.[26, 27]

LOCK IT IN:

Words aren't always required to move forward. Step, walk, breathe, let motion do the sorting. *Direction shows up once you take the first step.*

24 | Read this when *you're mentally checked out mid-shift*

BURNOUT BAIT:

You're physically present, but mentally off-grid. The call's happening, the radio's talking, the world's still moving, but you're somewhere else. Zoned out. Fogged up. Checked out.

TACTICAL TRADE-OFF:

FLUID RESET SEQUENCE

- Roll your shoulders back. Stretch your jaw. Tilt your head left, then right.
- Then take one deep breath through your nose. Long exhale through your mouth.
- Lock It In: *"Eyes up. Locked in. Stay sharp. This matters."*

That's your switch. Back to now.

WHY THIS WORKS:

Targeted movement plus clear internal direction helps snap you out of the mental fog. You're giving your body and brain a way to sync back up... fast.[28]

LOCK IT IN:

Fog will swallow you if you let it. Break it now, roll the tension out, breathe deep, dial in. Back in the fight. *Discipline is showing up in full, right where you stand.*

25 | Read this when *your energy is gone before the day starts*

BURNOUT BAIT:

Your default might be to fake it till caffeine hits. Start low, stay low. Scroll. Grumble. Walk in already bracing for impact. The day owns you before you even get to your gear.

TACTICAL TRADE-OFF:

Jumpstart Sequence

- Bounce in place, like a boxer in the ring, for at least 30 seconds.
- Then chug 8 oz of water. No sipping.
- Mentally lock in:

"Wake it up. Flush it out. Let's go."

WHY THIS WORKS:

Bouncing boosts circulation and water kick-starts alertness. Together they switch your system out of shutdown and into gear.[29, 30]

LOCK IT IN:

Dragging through the morning doesn't serve you. Wake the body, fuel it, and choose your pace. ***Readiness is built, not borrowed.***

26 | Read this when *you feel invisible*

BURNOUT BAIT:

You might default to isolation. Keep your head down. Stay busy. You want to be seen, but not if it means being judged or exposed. So, you hold back, even when you need support.

TACTICAL TRADE-OFF:

LET THE LIGHT IN

When someone offers you support, a check-in, a compliment, a simple "you good?" don't block it. Don't downplay. Just let it land.

Even if it's awkward. Even if it's brief.

Receiving doesn't make you weak. It makes you real.

WHY THIS WORKS:

Letting support land activates your body's social safety system. Even small moments of being seen help lower stress and rebuild trust.[31]

LOCK IT IN:

Being unseen doesn't make you less real. Let the light land when it comes, don't block it. *Visibility starts with permission... yours.*

27 | Read this when *you're holding it together by tuning out*

BURNOUT BAIT:

Your default might be to mentally check out just enough to stay functional. Not present, not gone, just floating. Background noise gets louder than your own thoughts, and you ride it to survive the shift.

TACTICAL TRADE-OFF:

SOUND ANCHOR + RETURN

- Pick one sound, AC hum, dispatch traffic, hallway movement.

- Track it for 10-15 seconds. Don't analyze it, just follow it.

- Then shift your eyes. Slowly scan your space while you listen for two more sounds.

- Once you've tracked three, take one deep breath.

- Lock back into one task. You're back in the game, on your terms.

WHY THIS WORKS:

Tuning into a steady sound helps your brain connect with the moment, and adding eye movement pulls you back from disconnection, without forcing focus.[32]

LOCK IT IN:

Tuning out keeps you functional but distant. Anchor with sound, scan with sight, and reset control. *Presence is a weapon, keep it sharp.*

28 | **Read this when** *you're spaced-out during conversations*

BURNOUT BAIT:

Your default might be to drift. You're nodding, standing there, doing all the right things, but your brain's somewhere else. You're not disengaged on purpose. You just can't lock in.

TACTICAL TRADE-OFF:

EYE CONTACT ANCHOR

• Hold their gaze, three full seconds.

• Watch their face. Let yourself *really* see them.

• As you do, drop your shoulders. Unclench your jaw.

• This isn't a threat. It's a conversation. Let your body know it's safe to stay.

WHY THIS WORKS:

Eye contact plus softening signals safety to your nervous system. It shifts you out of survival mode and into real-time connection, without forcing words.[33]

LOCK IT IN:

Connection starts in the eyes. Hold steady, drop the tension, and stay in the room. *Focus is respect, give it, and you strengthen both of you.*

29 | Read this when *you feel stuck and nothing stirs in you*

BURNOUT BAIT:

Your default might be to keep moving through the same loop, same routes, same routines, same blankness. You're not falling apart. You're just stuck. Numb. Disconnected from anything that used to spark something in you.

TACTICAL TRADE-OFF:

MEMORY TAP DRILL

- Tap the center of your chest with two fingers, steady rhythm.

- Pull up one real memory: a laugh you couldn't hold in, a win that hit deep, a moment you felt fully alive.

- Play it for five seconds.

You're not faking it. You're reconnecting with proof that you can still feel.

WHY THIS WORKS:

Tapping while recalling a meaningful moment activates emotion through your senses. Your body often remembers how to feel before your mind does, and that evidence pulls you forward.[34]

LOCK IT IN:

Stuck is a signal, not an end state. Tap in, pull up a spark, and bring yourself back online. *Don't wait for life to return, call it forward.*

Read this when you're
Overwhelmed

Calls stacking. Reports half-done. Evidence waiting to be entered. Charges that needed to be filed yesterday. Dispatch asking for updates. My phone buzzing with texts I didn't even have the bandwidth to read. And then the computer froze up. Screen locked, work gone, time wasted. That was it. That was the shove.

I was alone in the squad room when I grabbed my metal clipboard and sent it flying. My jaw was locked. Shoulders burning. Heart pounding like I was gearing up for a fight even though I was just sitting there. My thoughts scattered, part of me trying to keep track of the checklist, part of me wanting to walk out, part of me just blank. That frozen screen lit the fuse. Petty, sure. But it was still the least of what I wanted to do.

These entries are for when your body is already maxed, your brain scrambles, and the smallest thing becomes the outlet. Not to make it all disappear, but to give you tactical ways to carve out enough space to breathe. Enough clarity to stop the spin. Enough control to take one step instead of sinking under the weight of all of it.

30 | Read this when *you're completely overstimulated*

BURNOUT BAIT:

You shut down. Snap at the wrong person. Or bulldoze through, hoping if you just move faster, the noise will stop. You're fried, and your system's flooding, but you keep going like nothing's wrong.

TACTICAL TRADE-OFF:

3-POINT RESET: PRESSURE. POSTURE. PERIPHERY

- Grip something solid... your vest strap, steering wheel, pen.
- Lift your spine one inch taller.
- Without turning your head, scan your side vision and name one fixed object in each direction.

This is not zoning out, it's pulling yourself back in.

WHY THIS WORKS:

Grip, posture, and side-vision scanning give your body strong grounding signals. This anchors you in the moment and calms sensory overload.[35]

LOCK IT IN:

Stacked noise will bury you unless you break it. Anchor down, rise tall, scan wide, and reset your ground. *Command cuts through chaos every time.*

31 | Read this when *you're drowning in to-dos and expectations*

BURNOUT BAIT:

You push harder. Try to knock out five things at once. You say yes to another ask, even though you're already maxed. The urge is to sprint through it all and hope it calms down on the other side—but it never does.

TACTICAL TRADE-OFF:

RUN A 5-MINUTE COMMAND SWEEP

- Step back. Imagine you're incident command on your own mental scene.

- What's an actual threat? What's just noise?

- Call out your next *three clear moves* out loud or on paper.

You don't need to do it all. You need to take control of the scene.

WHY THIS WORKS:

Running a quick command sweep uses the same skills you rely on in the field... assess, prioritize, act. Speaking your next moves out loud locks your brain into execution instead of overwhelm.[36]

LOCK IT IN:

Chaos will run you if you don't run it. Step back, sweep the scene, and call your next three moves out loud. *Clarity is your weapon, aim it, and fire.*

32 | **Read this when *you want to scream or disappear***

BURNOUT BAIT:

You grit your teeth. Slam a door. Snap at someone who didn't deserve it. Or you vanish, quiet, quit the moment, emotionally check out, or leave before you lose it. Either way, you're trying to get relief without wreckage.

TACTICAL TRADE-OFF:

MICRO-EXIT + RE-ENTRY PLAN

- Excuse yourself for 60 seconds or longer if you can, restroom, hallway, supply room. If not, turn away and put both hands on something steady.

- On your way back in, lock onto one small task. Not the whole scene. Just the next piece.

You're not bailing. You're buying yourself control.

WHY THIS WORKS:

A short step away stops overload from spilling out. Coming back with one small task resets focus and puts you back in control.[37]

LOCK IT IN:

The urge to blow up or vanish is a signal, not a command. Step out, steady, and re-enter on your terms. ***Reset buys you control when the moment tries to take it.***

33 | Read this when *you can't take one more question, noise, or task*

BURNOUT BAIT:

You hit that internal wall where every sound grates and every ask feels like an attack. You might lash out, shut down, or fake your way through, but you're past capacity, and the system's still loading.

TACTICAL TRADE-OFF:

BARE-MINIMUM + BRIEF OUT LOUD

Say one line to set the boundary:

- "Give me a sec, my brain's full."
- "Not ignoring, just maxed, stand by."
- "Hang tight, I need a second to track."
- Then shift into bare-minimum ops: One task. Minimal talk. No extras.

Buy yourself space without disappearing.

WHY THIS WORKS:

Saying your limit out loud lowers pressure and keeps others from misreading you. Pairing it with bare-minimum tasks protects your focus until capacity comes back.

LOCK IT IN:

Capacity has limits, pretending it doesn't will bury you. Mark the line, strip it down to essentials, and reclaim your ground. *Holding the line starts with holding your own.*

34 | Read this when *the details keep slipping through*

BURNOUT BAIT:

You try to stay on top of it, but things keep falling apart. You forget a follow-up. Miss a deadline. Overlook a detail. You're busy, but not effective, and now the weight of what you're missing is piling up fast.

TACTICAL TRADE-OFF:

LIST TO LOCATE

This won't fix everything in five minutes, but it'll stop the freefall.

Grab your phone or paper and make two quick lists:

- What's already done
- What still needs to be handled

Don't overthink it. Just externalize it.

You can't fix what you can't see.

WHY THIS WORKS:

Overload clogs working memory. Writing down what's done and what's left clears mental space and gives you back a sense of control.

LOCK IT IN:

Your head can't hold it all. Dump it fast, sort it clean, and see what's real. *Control starts by getting it out where you can see it.*

35 | **Read this when** *the pressure is physically making you ill*

BURNOUT BAIT:

You keep pushing through the fog. The tight chest. The rolling stomach. You tell yourself to suck it up, but your body's throwing the brakes. You feel like you might snap, puke, or vanish, and you're trying to act normal through it.

TACTICAL TRADE-OFF:

TARGETED PRESSURE POINT RESET

- Press firmly into the web between your thumb and index finger.
- Hold for 30 seconds. Switch hands.
- Then press three finger-widths below your wrist on the inner forearm.

Do both sides. One at a time. Breathe while you press.

WHY THIS WORKS:

These pressure points help settle your nervous system. They calm nausea, drop adrenaline, and give your body a signal to downshift before it crashes.[38]

LOCK IT IN:

Your body's throwing red flags you can't afford to ignore. Hit the pressure points, breathe, and reset before it stacks higher. *Relief is a skill, use it before the pressure owns you.*

36 | Read this when *you can't figure out what to do first*

BURNOUT BAIT:

You freeze. Or you default to busywork just to feel in motion. Everything feels urgent. Everyone needs something. You bounce between half-started tasks, and the longer you stall, the heavier it all feels.

TACTICAL TRADE-OFF:

CLEAR THE CRITICAL PATH.

Ask: What's the thing that gets someone else stuck if I don't move?

Start there.

Then pick one thing that clears your own runway next.

Don't chase the loudest task, clear the one that unlocks the rest.

WHY THIS WORKS:

Stress makes every task feel urgent. Identifying the one task that unlocks progress resets your sense of order and gets momentum back on track.

LOCK IT IN:

Freeze wastes more time than the wrong move ever will. Clear the critical path, knock it down, and open your runway. *Momentum starts with the task that unlocks the rest.*

37 | Read this when *your head and heart won't agree*

BURNOUT BAIT:

You try to logic your way through something emotional, or you drown in feelings you can't explain. You swing between overthinking and shutting down. Neither side wins, and you stay stuck in the middle.

TACTICAL TRADE-OFF:

LIST FOR CLARITY

This isn't something you'll solve in five minutes. But you can start moving.

Open your phone or grab paper.

Make two quick lists:

- What I know (facts, decisions, tasks)
- What I feel (frustrations, fears, gut stuff)

You don't have to fix it. Just separate it, so it stops spinning in one big knot.

WHY THIS WORKS:

Separating facts from feelings stops them from tangling together. It calms overwhelm and shows what can be acted on versus what just needs space.

LOCK IT IN:

Logic and emotion don't need to fight for the mic. Separate them, sort them, and move one piece at a time. *Order creates space, and space makes the next step possible.*

38 | Read this when *the smallest thing just broke you*

BURNOUT BAIT:

You snap. Slam a drawer. Say something you didn't mean. Or you shut down completely and pretend you're fine. The reaction feels too big for the moment, but your system's been holding back a tidal wave, and that tiny thing just cracked the dam.

TACTICAL TRADE-OFF:

OVERRIDE THE OVERWHELM

- Touch four different textures around you, fabric, metal, plastic, skin.
- Feel each one for a few seconds. Focus only on how it feels.
- Then take three slow, steady breaths.

Let your body register safety before your brain makes a decision.

WHY THIS WORKS:

Paying attention to texture pulls focus from emotion to the sense in the body. Adding slow breaths steadies the system and lowers the intensity in the system.

LOCK IT IN:

When the stack blows over the edge, don't overthink it. Grab the room with your senses, take three breaths, and get your feet back under you. *Hold the ground, don't hand it over.*

39 | Read this when *you're about to rage-quit everything*

BURNOUT BAIT:

You start writing the resignation text in your head. You imagine walking out, blocking the number, deleting the thread. You don't want a resolution... you want out. The urge to blow it all up feels like the only way to breathe.

TACTICAL TRADE-OFF:

HIT RECORD, CHECK THE SCRIPT

Grab your phone. Open the camera. Film a 30-second rant, say exactly what you want to say.

Then watch it back. Would you stand by those words if someone else said them? Would you be proud to hit send?

And if you can't bring yourself to film it... that's the clearest sign you're not in the headspace to decide anything.

WHY THIS WORKS:

Recording your words pulls the reaction out of your head. Watching it back gives distance, which makes space for wiser choices.

LOCK IT IN:

Burning it all down feels like freedom, but it's just fallout. Get it out, hear it back, and decide from a distance. *Decisions carry weight, make them from wisdom, not combustion.*

Read this when
Your Mind is Spinning

I've sat frozen in front of a screen, a simple task waiting, and my brain refusing to grab onto anything solid. Thoughts pulled in one after another until they blurred together. If I started here, I'd drop the ball there. If I did that, I'd forget the first thing. Time disappeared, and all I had was a locked jaw, shallow breaths, and nerves buzzing like live wires.

This wasn't outside pressure, no radio blaring, no calls stacking, no one demanding anything. It was all inside. A tornado in my own head. From the outside, it looks fierce, all energy and power. On the inside, it's whiplash. You're getting tossed around, slammed from angle to angle, with nothing steady to hold onto. The harder you try to wrestle it, the more it throws you.

These entries are for when the noise is coming from the inside. Quick, practical ways to interrupt the cycle, create space in the middle of the storm, and get yourself moving again. Not perfection, not total silence, just enough traction to break loose and take the next step.

40 | Read this when *your brain won't quit running worst-case*

BURNOUT BAIT:

Your default might be to forecast catastrophe, rehearse worst-case scenarios, or mentally brace for impact that hasn't happened. You call it being prepared, but your body's reacting like it's already happening. You're trained for chaos, but this is overload, not readiness.

TACTICAL TRADE-OFF:

BREAK THE PATTERN DRILL

Interrupt the loop with something unfamiliar. Take a different route. Grab coffee somewhere new. Switch up your playlist. Rearrange your gear. You're not avoiding the hard stuff; you're reminding your brain it's not stuck in threat mode. Disrupt the drill so you can return with clarity.

WHY THIS WORKS:

Switching up a routine gives your brain proof it's not locked in threat mode. That small change disrupts the loop and restores focus.[39]

LOCK IT IN:

Worst-case rehearsals drain you before the fight even shows up. Break the pattern, disrupt the loop, and prove you're adaptable. *Readiness is calm under pressure, not creating chaos before it.*

41 | Read this when *you're second-guessing every move you made*

BURNOUT BAIT:

Your default might be to loop the footage in your head, obsess over tone, timing, or things you wish you'd said. You're not learning from the moment...you're punishing yourself with it.

TACTICAL TRADE-OFF:

60-SECOND AAR

Run a 60-second AAR. What was the situation? What did you know at the time? What action did you take? What's one thing you'll carry forward? Keep it brief. Keep it real. And then close with this truth: *If it could have gone any other way, it would have.*

WHY THIS WORKS:

A quick AAR shifts replay into structure. It closes the loop, cuts off rumination, and reinforces trust in your decisions under pressure.[40]

LOCK IT IN:

Replays drain energy. Strip it down to facts, take the lesson, and close the book. *Confidence grows when you finish the review and walk forward.*

42 | Read this when *you keep solving problems that aren't yours*

BURNOUT BAIT:

Your default might be to take on too much, fixing things for people who never asked, anticipating needs that aren't yours to meet, or absorbing stress that doesn't belong to you. You tell yourself you're just helping, but underneath is the belief that it's your job to hold it all.

TACTICAL TRADE-OFF:

DRAW THE LINE IN INK

Draw the damn line. On paper. Right now. Split a page in two: *Theirs* and *Mine*. No overthinking. No sugarcoating. Write it all out. What's actually yours to handle? What's not? Clarity cuts the weight in half. And protecting your capacity is a top tier strategy.

WHY THIS WORKS:

Writing out what's yours versus what's not gives your brain a clear boundary. That external line stops the overload of carrying everyone else's weight.

LOCK IT IN:

Over-carrying kills capacity. Split the page, draw the line, and own what's yours. ***Boundaries sharpen focus and keep your focus clean.***

43 | Read this when *your brain won't shut the hell up*

BURNOUT BAIT:

Your default might be to spiral in silence, fill the space with noise, or try to outthink the overthinking. But the more you chase quiet, the louder it gets. You're not solving anything; you're just feeding the loop.

TACTICAL TRADE-OFF:

GIVE THE NOISE A JOB

Give your brain something *boring but structured* to do. Count backward from 100 by threes. Read road signs out loud. Name objects in the room by category, vehicles, colors, brands. Thought spirals need friction.

WHY THIS WORKS:

Giving your brain a simple, structured task interrupts rumination. The focus shift acts like brakes and slows the spiral.[41]

LOCK IT IN:

Spirals need friction to stop. Give your mind a task, simple and steady, until the noise breaks pace. *Your mind will follow the lane you build, build one that sharpens you.*

44 | Read this when *even the simplest choices feel impossible*

BURNOUT BAIT:

Your default might be to stall out, overthink every option, or crowdsource answers you already know. You're not indecisive... you're depleted. When everything feels like too much, even choosing what to eat can feel like a trap.

TACTICAL TRADE-OFF:

FLIP THE DEFAULT

Pick the opposite of what you usually would. Grab the thing you never reach for. Choose the road you don't normally take. Stop looking for the right call, and just make a call. Your system doesn't need perfection. It needs momentum.

WHY THIS WORKS:

Doing something different breaks indecision loops. Novelty reboots flexibility and reminds your brain it can still adapt.[42]

LOCK IT IN:

Freeze feeds fatigue. Flip the script, make the call, and prove to yourself the world doesn't end on a single choice. *Progress is built by decisions in motion, not decisions delayed.*

45 | Read this when *you're zoning out mid-task or convo*

BURNOUT BAIT:

Your default might be to fake your way through it, nod, say "yep," or keep working while your brain floats three steps behind. You're physically there, but your focus keeps slipping just far enough to miss what matters. It's not a motivation problem; it's a system running on fumes.

TACTICAL TRADE-OFF:

60 SECOND CLARITY RESET

Step away from the task for sixty seconds. Set a timer if you need to. No scrolling. No multitasking. Stand still, look at a blank wall, or walk a small loop. Let your mind clear. When the minute's up, return and name your next move out loud. This is a discipline reset, not a distraction.

WHY THIS WORKS:

A short, intentional pause clears mental clutter. That reset lowers load and sharpens focus when you return.

LOCK IT IN:

Presence slips when the system is overloaded. Step out for sixty seconds, clear the fog, then come back sharp. *Attention sharpens when you cut the static instead of swimming in it.*

46 | **Read this when *your thoughts are all static***

BURNOUT BAIT:

Your default might be to power through, distract yourself, or hope the fog clears on its own. But mental static isn't silence, it's unfiltered noise jamming your clarity. You're not broken; you're just overloaded with nowhere to channel it.

TACTICAL TRADE-OFF:

CREATE A CLEAN SIGNAL

Find or make a steady rhythm. Tap your thigh in a four-count. Match your breath to your steps. Hum a low note under your breath. You're not just calming down, you're taking command. Give your brain something real to sync with so it stops chewing on chaos.

WHY THIS WORKS:

Locking into rhythm organizes scattered firing in the brain. A steady beat pulls your system into order and calms mental noise.

AFFIRM IT:

Static isn't silence, it's a wasted signal. Give it rhythm, give it form, and make it carry you forward. *A steady beat can punch through the fuzz.*

47 | Read this when *you feel mentally slow and fogged out*

BURNOUT BAIT:

Your default might be to grab more caffeine, zone out, or try to power through with a half-working brain. But that fog isn't just fatigue, it's a backlog of unprocessed noise your system can't sort fast enough.

TACTICAL TRADE-OFF:

CHANGE YOUR COORDINATES

Stand if you're sitting. Sit if you've been standing. Drop to a knee. Step up on something. Shift your physical position, and then change your line of sight. Look high, low, or sideways. You're not just moving your body; you're recalibrating your mental grid. New angles clear new paths.

WHY THIS WORKS:

Changing posture and viewpoint reactivates your sensory system. That shift refreshes attention and helps clear mental haze.

LOCK IT IN:

Fog means the system's jammed, not finished. Shift your stance, lift your line of sight, pull a deep breath, and change the channel. *One sharp adjustment can cut through more haze than an hour of pushing harder.*

48 | Read this when *you're overanalyzing every conversation*

BURNOUT BAIT:

Your default might be to replay every pause, every look, every word, convinced you missed something, said too much, or made it weird. You're not reflecting, you're reliving. And it's burning brainpower you don't owe it.

TACTICAL TRADE-OFF:

SEAL THE DEBRIEF

- Stand up. Brush your hands across each shoulder three times...left, right, left, right, left, right.

- Then swipe down each arm like you're brushing off dirt.

- Finish with one swipe down the chest. Say it out loud: "*That moment is complete.*" Move like you mean it. Let your body clear what your brain's still clinging to.

WHY THIS WORKS:

Physical closure helps your system release tension and stop the mental loop. Moving with intention gives your brain a new command.[43]

LOCK IT IN:

Overthinking keeps you tethered to what's already gone. Cut the line and claim the ground you're standing on. *The present is the only place you have command.*

Read this when you're
Emotionally Flooded

Even when I was burning out, on scene, I could lock it down and do the job. That part came naturally. But later, when the noise was gone, it would catch me off guard. And then it blindsided me when I least expected it. No neat label. No warning. Just a surge that knocked me sideways.

It didn't come in order, and it never matched the moment. I thought I was fine, and then my gut would tighten, my throat would close, or my vision would blur. Tears I didn't want but couldn't stop. Anger I couldn't explain. A heaviness that sat on my chest like it belonged there.

That's what happens when you keep pushing everything down to get through. It doesn't stay buried. It waits, and when it breaks the surface, it comes fast.

This section is here for those moments, when the feelings don't line up, when they hit harder than you expect, and when you're not sure what to do with them. These entries will help you steady when the flood comes, let it move without swallowing you, and come out the other side able to breathe again.

49 | **Read this when *you're about to cry and don't know why***

BURNOUT BAIT:

You try to suck it up, shake it off, or blink the tears away like always. But your body knows. It's carrying something words haven't caught up to yet.

TACTICAL TRADE-OFF:

STERNUM + COLLARBONE TAP

Start by gently tapping the center of your chest (sternum) with two fingers, steady rhythm. After 10 seconds, begin tapping along your collarbones, just beneath the clavicle, left to right, then back again. Keep breathing. Let the wave pass.

WHY THIS WORKS:

Tapping the chest and collarbones sends steady sensory input through the body. That rhythm helps regulate emotion and eases the buildup.[44]

LOCK IT IN:

When emotion blindsides you, don't choke it down. Tap it out, breathe steady, and let your body cycle it through. ***Release keeps you mission-ready when holding it in would jam the system.***

FLOODED

50 | **Read this when** *you're feeling everything all at once*

BURNOUT BAIT:

You either bottle it up or blow it out sideways. Every emotion's fighting for airtime, and you're the only one on duty. No wonder your system is fried.

TACTICAL TRADE-OFF:

SHOULDER ROLL + STACKED BREATH

- Drop your arms.
- Roll your shoulders up, back, and down. Slow and steady. As you do, take one deep breath into your belly, then one into your chest.
- Exhale slow. Do five rounds.

Let the tension peel off.

WHY THIS WORKS:

Rolling the shoulders releases stored tension, while stacked breathing regulates the system. Together they calm intensity without needing a full fix.[45]

LOCK IT IN:

Stacked emotions don't need sorting, they need space. Let the breath widen, let the dust settle. *Steadiness makes room for the rest to land.*

FLOODED

51 | **Read this when *grief hits out of nowhere***

BURNOUT BAIT:

You lock it down, swallow the lump, and pretend nothing happened. You call it random, but your body remembers what your brain buried. Grief shows up unannounced, not to wreck you, but to remind you that something mattered.

TACTICAL TRADE-OFF:

PALM PRESS + SILENT HONOR

Press your palm flat against the center of your chest. Apply gentle pressure. Breathe into the resistance. Let the moment rise. No fixing. No hiding. Just witness it. If emotion leaks out, let it. It might be just the release you need.

WHY THIS WORKS:

Pressing your palm to your chest gives grounding input to the body. Breathing with it instead of shutting it down lets grief move through naturally.[46]

LOCK IT IN:

When it blindsides you, don't choke it down. Palm to chest, steady breath, let it rise and move through. *Grief marks what was sacred, carry it forward as testament, not as chains.*

52 | **Read this when** *you're holding someone else's pain*

BURNOUT BAIT:

You nod, absorb, and tell yourself to be strong for them. You don't want them to feel alone, so you carry it, quietly, fully, and without question. But now it's lodged in your chest like it's yours.

TACTICAL TRADE-OFF:

SHAKE + SPEAK RELEASE

Stand or sit. Shake out your hands, like you're flicking water off your fingertips.

- Then say, out loud or in your head: *I witnessed it. I supported it. But I don't have to keep it.*
- Do three rounds. Shake. Speak. Breathe.

WHY THIS WORKS:

Shaking your hands discharges built-up tension. Pairing it with a release phrase creates separation so your body stops carrying what isn't yours.[47]

LOCK IT IN:

You can witness without carrying. Shake it out, breathe it through, and return it to where it belongs. *Compassion can hold space; it doesn't have to chain you to the weight.*

53 | Read this when *you're sad but still have to show up*

BURNOUT BAIT:

You shove the sadness down, slap on the uniform, and tell yourself there's no room for it right now. You stay functional, but the ache sits just under the surface, waiting for a crack to leak through.

TACTICAL TRADE-OFF:

FRICTION RESET

- Rub your palms together hard until heat builds.
- Press that warmth into the sides of your face or the back of your neck.
- Hold for three steady breaths.
- Tell yourself: *"I'll come back to this later."*

You're not erasing the sadness, just giving your body enough relief to keep moving until you have space to face it.

WHY THIS WORKS:

Friction heat gives your body a quick grounding cue. Pairing it with breath creates a pause, and promising to return keeps sadness contained instead of buried.[48]

LOCK IT IN:

Sadness doesn't vanish because you're on duty. Buy yourself a pocket of relief, mark it for later, and move forward steady. Pause now, return when you've got the space. *The weight can wait; your presence can't.*

54 | Read this when *guilt creeps in*

BURNOUT BAIT:

You over-apologize. Overthink. You keep replaying that one moment, whether it was a real misstep or just a story your nervous system made up. Either way, guilt grabs the mic and won't shut up.

TACTICAL TRADE-OFF:

FINGER TAP REASSURANCE

Touch each fingertip to your thumb, one at a time. As you do, say: Let that shit go. Repeat three cycles. Let breath lead. If you messed up, own it. If you didn't, stop bleeding energy into it. Either way, you get to move forward.

WHY THIS WORKS:

Finger tapping gives your body rhythm to settle the spiral. Pairing it with a release phrase directs your brain to drop the guilt and reset.[49]

LOCK IT IN:

Tap it out, breathe it through, and speak truth into it. If it's yours, own it and adjust. If it's not, stop feeding it. *Guilt fades when discipline takes its place.*

55 | Read this when *you're ashamed of how much it hurts*

BURNOUT BAIT:

You try to rationalize it. Downplay it. You tell yourself, "This shouldn't hurt this bad," and then pile shame on top of pain. You push through, embarrassed it even got to you in the first place.

TACTICAL TRADE-OFF:

PAIN INVENTORY

What did this pain leave behind?

Not because it was worth it. Not because it was noble. But because it happened.

List what you've learned, from this moment, from this weight, from this wound. Say it or write it. Then ask: *What's available to me now that wasn't before?* Clarity? Compassion? Boundaries? Strength? Let the evidence speak.

WHY THIS WORKS:

Listing what the pain left behind reframes it as information instead of failure. That shift breaks the shame loop and shows what can be carried forward.[50]

LOCK IT IN:

Pain doesn't need excuses. Face it head-on, strip out the shame, and let it stand. *This hurt is evidence you're still alive to the things that matter.*

56 | Read this when *your anger wants to take over*

BURNOUT BAIT:

You want to yell, throw something, or walk until your legs give out. The energy's crawling under your skin, and there's no clean way to let it out. So, you either explode, or implode.

TACTICAL TRADE-OFF:

FORCE EXHALE + SILENT ROAR

Clench your fists. Inhale through your nose. Then open your mouth wide and exhale hard, but silent, like a roar you're holding back. Do it again. Then again. Let your face scrunch. Let your body feel it. You're not swallowing the anger; you're letting it move.

FLOODED

WHY THIS WORKS:

A forceful, silent exhale gives anger a physical release without causing damage. It lets your system offload intensity instead of storing it.[51]

LOCK IT IN:

Clench, exhale, let it move without landing on anyone else. *Anger is fuel, direct it where it builds, not where it burns.*

57 | Read this when *the emotions are stuck and need to move*

BURNOUT BAIT:

You freeze. You scroll. You go numb and hope something snaps you out of it. But the more you wait, the heavier it gets, and the harder it is to start moving again.

TACTICAL TRADE-OFF:

MICRO-MOVE CHAIN

Pick one hand or foot. Move it gently. Then move the next joint it connects to, wrist or ankle. Then elbow or knee. Then shoulder or hip. Keep going until you reach the center. Then reverse the chain, one joint at a time, back out. Let motion restart the signal.

WHY THIS WORKS:

Moving one joint at a time gives your system a sequence to follow. That chain reaction restarts flow and brings the body back online.[52]

LOCK IT IN:

If nothing's breaking through, don't wait it out, strike the spark yourself. *Even the slightest ignition reminds you you're still alive in here.*

58 | Read this when *you're not allowed to break, but want to*

BURNOUT BAIT:

You hold it in. You hold it all. You tell yourself, "Not here. Not now." So, you stuff it down and keep functioning, but inside, you're begging for a safe place to unravel.

TACTICAL TRADE-OFF:

SCHEDULE THE BREAKDOWN

- If you can't break right now... *book it*. Name the time. Pick the place. "Tonight, after the kids are in bed." "When I get back to the station." "After tomorrow's shift." Put it on the mental calendar like anything else that matters.

- Give yourself the promise of space. You'll show up better when you stop pretending you don't need to fall apart.

WHY THIS WORKS:

Delaying is different than denying. When your brain knows there's a plan for release, it stops clenching like it has to hold forever.[53]

LOCK IT IN:

Put the release on the clock so your brain stops clamping down like it has to hold forever. Discipline means knowing when to fight and when to fall back. *Strong leaders plan the offload too.*

Read this when
The Job Bleeds into Your Life

There was a stretch when I was technically home, but only long enough to rinse off the shift, catch a few hours of sleep, and head back out. One night, around 2 a.m., I ended up on the couch eating cereal out of a leaf-shaped Thanksgiving gravy boat. Every dish in the house was dirty. I wasn't keeping up with the basics. I was distracted by the job, battling depression between shifts, and forgetting what it meant to actually live.

That's when it hit me, I had turned my life into a pit stop.

This section isn't just about burnout on the job. It's about how the job creeps into everything else. Your tone. Your pace. Your presence. It's not always loud or dramatic, but it builds. And if you don't catch it, it starts stealing from the parts of your life that actually matter.

These entries are here to help you spot the bleed-over, and shift it. Not perfectly. Not all at once. One moment, one adjustment, one choice at a time.

59 | Read this when *you can't switch out of responder mode*

BURNOUT BAIT:

You're still scanning. Still solving. Still waiting for the call that isn't coming. You bark orders at home like you're clearing a scene. Your tone's clipped. Your body's braced. You're stuck in duty tempo, even when the duty is done.

TACTICAL TRADE-OFF:

SWITCH THE CHANNEL

Treat your transition like a ritual. Turn off the noise that keeps you on alert. Put on music that slows your pulse. Change the lighting... use a lamp, crack a window, ditch the overheads. Swap your shirt. Kick off your boots. Wash your hands. Splash your face. Let your body know: we're not on shift anymore.

WHY THIS WORKS:

Your nervous system tracks cues, not clocks. Changing sensory inputs helps your brain exit responder mode and re-enter real life.[54]

LOCK IT IN:

Your system's still running hot, even when the call is over. Change the channel on purpose, sound, pace, light, gear. Give your body the cue to stand down. *Precision isn't lost in the reset, it's sharpened there.*

60 | Read this when *your family gets the leftovers*

BURNOUT BAIT:

You gave your best energy to the call, the shift, the chaos. By the time you walk through your front door, there's nothing left in the tank. So, they get the scraps, the sighs, the silence, the shutdown.

TACTICAL TRADE-OFF:

FRONT-LOAD THE FIRST FIVE

Before you check out, check in.

- Offer five minutes of undivided attention to the people you care about, no phone, no TV, no multitasking.
- Look them in the eye. Be fully there, even briefly.
- Then take your buffer time, knowing you've laid the groundwork to come back and reconnect.

WHY THIS WORKS:

A few minutes of full attention rebuilds connection fast. It sets trust for them and eases your transition home.[55]

LOCK IT IN:

Don't save what's left, set the tone with what you've got. Five minutes of undivided presence lays a foundation they can count on, even if you're spent. *Give them the first cut, not the scraps.*

61 | **Read this when** *the call is still living in your head*

BURNOUT BAIT:

You're off shift, but the scene's still running on a loop. What you saw. What you missed. What you wish you said. You try to shake it off, but it clings. You're back in it without meaning to be.

TACTICAL TRADE-OFF:

NAME. FRAME. CONTAIN.

- Say it out loud or write it down: "That call's over, but my body still feels like it's happening."
- Frame it... was it hard, haunting, heavy? Then contain it.
- Visualize placing the memory in a strong, sealed container. Bookmark it for later.

You're not ignoring it...you're choosing when and how to revisit it, maybe with someone trained to help carry the weight.

WHY THIS WORKS:

Naming the memory engages clear thinking. Framing it gives context, and containing it stops the replay so you decide when to revisit it.[56]

LOCK IT IN:

Put the memory in a container you choose, words, paper, a mental box. Mark it as closed until you have the space and support to reopen it. *Seal it before it bleeds into the next moment, reopen it at the first real opportunity.*

62 | Read this when *you're more comfortable at work than at home*

BURNOUT BAIT:

You keep reaching for the uniform. Signing up for one more shift. Not because you need the money, but because the job makes sense. You know who you are there. At home, it's quieter but harder. You feel untethered, unsure, out of place. So, you run back to the chaos that feels like control.

TACTICAL TRADE-OFF:

RECLAIM A CIVILIAN RITUAL

• Pick one thing that has *nothing* to do with the job.

• Light a candle. Change into real clothes. Sit on the porch with a drink in your hand and no radio on your hip.

• Let your body practice being off-duty. Let the discomfort come, and pass.

WHY THIS WORKS:

Your system holds on to what feels familiar. Simple home-based rituals retrain it to recognize off-duty space and ease the shift in identity.

LOCK IT IN:

Create a signal that shifts you out of uniform, change the clothes, change the light, change the tempo. Let your body know this space matters. *Come all the way home, not just through the door.*

63 | **Read this when *you're feeling numb with your kids***

BURNOUT BAIT:

You shut down even more. Numb out on your phone. Fake a smile and hope it passes. Or worse, you snap just to feel something. The guilt hits after, but the pattern repeats. Disengagement, regret, repeat.

TACTICAL TRADE-OFF:

ENGAGE ONE SENSE

Pick one of your senses and plug back in. Hold their hand and really feel it. Smell their hair. Name three colors in the room out loud. Then offer one small act of connection, a question, a compliment, a hug. You don't have to feel lit up to show up.

WHY THIS WORKS:

Numbness is the body's freeze response. Sensory input interrupts it and helps you re-engage in the moment.

LOCK IT IN:

Pick one sense and lock into it, their hand in yours, their laugh, the colors around you. Small anchors pull you back into the moment. *Connection is built in presence, not perfection.*

64 | Read this when *everything off-duty feels too "soft"*

BURNOUT BAIT:

You chase adrenaline off the clock. You double down on high-output hobbies, overtrain at the gym, or pick fights just to feel something real. You avoid stillness, tell yourself you're just wired this way, but all it's doing is keeping your system on edge and burning you out faster.

TACTICAL TRADE-OFF:

GO HARD THEN GO HOME

Do something physically intense *on purpose*, push-ups, a sprint, a cold shower. Let your system burn off the edge. Then follow it up with something grounding, even if it's just 60 seconds of stillness. Use the intensity as a bridge, not a lifestyle.

WHY THIS WORKS:

Your body can't jump straight from high alert to calm. Burning off intensity first makes it easier to settle into grounding afterward.

LOCK IT IN:

Hit the gas on purpose, then ease off. Sprint, push, or plunge cold, then stand still and let your system reset. *Let intensity clear the path for the contentment that follows.*

65 | Read this when *your tone's still tactical at the dinner table*

BURNOUT BAIT:

You don't mean to sound sharp, but everything comes out clipped, commanding, or cold. You talk like you're clearing a scene. Correcting instead of connecting. Giving orders instead of answers. It's not what you say, it's how you're saying it. And it's pushing people away.

TACTICAL TRADE-OFF:

DROP IN, THEN SPEAK

Before you answer, pause. Feel your feet. Relax your jaw. Drop your shoulders an inch. Then respond, with warmth, not warning. Add one quick gratitude check-in: notice one thing you're thankful for in the room, the moment, or the person in front of you. It softens the edge and brings you back.

WHY THIS WORKS:

Your voice follows your body's state. Relaxing posture before you speak shifts tone and presence, making connection easier to reach.

LOCK IT IN:

Drop the command voice. Loosen the jaw, lower the shoulders, and answer like you're breaking bread, not clearing a scene. *Two-way respect at the table is what turns a house into home.*

CROSSOVER

66 | Read this when *your brain won't let the shift go*

BURNOUT BAIT:

You keep mentally clocking back in. Running through calls, second-guessing decisions, rechecking reports in your head. You feel like you *should* be off, but your mind keeps dragging you back on shift. It's not helpful. It's not productive. It's just keeping you activated.

TACTICAL TRADE-OFF:

THRESHOLD SHOWER

As you move through each doorway, into your house, your bedroom, the kitchen, imagine walking through a warm shower that washes off the shift. Let each threshold signal a reset. You're not dragging it with you. You're stepping into something clean.

WHY THIS WORKS:

Pairing movement with imagery gives your body a clear reset signal. Each threshold becomes a marker that the shift is finished.

AFFIRM IT:

Your body doesn't track time, it tracks signals. Show it the shift has ended with action, not thought. *The handoff isn't mental; it's marked in motion.*

67 | Read this when *you can't focus because you're still scanning for threats*

BURNOUT BAIT:

You're off duty, but your brain is still on. Watching exits. Tracking noise. Noticing things no one else even registers. You call it awareness, but it's more like being stuck in drive with nowhere to go. And it's bleeding into your personal life, conversations, dinners, and downtime. You're always half here, half somewhere else.

TACTICAL TRADE-OFF:

FLIP THE SCAN

If your brain's going to scan, redirect it with intention. Instead of threat-checking, scan for five signs of safety: a family photo, your kid's laugh, a locked door, warm food, the sound of the shower running. Turn your environment into proof that you're safe. Let your brain stand down.

WHY THIS WORKS:

Hypervigilance keeps your system on edge. Redirecting the scan toward signs of safety rewires the loop and helps your body stand down.[57]

LOCK IT IN:

Don't fight the scan, redirect it. Stack proof that you're safe until your system believes you. *Observe safety until you can absorb safety.*

68 | Read this when *you've forgotten how to just exist*

BURNOUT BAIT:

You fill every second. Scroll. Clean. Overtrain. Problem-solve. You sit still for five minutes and feel like you're wasting time. Doing nothing feels wrong. Like you're failing at being useful. So, you keep going, even when there's nowhere to go.

TACTICAL TRADE-OFF:

SET A TIMER AND STAY PUT

Three minutes. Sit. No phone. No to-do list. No fixing. Just stay where your feet are. Let your body fidget if it needs to. Let your thoughts pass without grabbing onto them. You're not failing, you're unlearning the habit of constant motion.

WHY THIS WORKS:

Constant motion wires your system to see stillness as wrong. Brief pauses teach your body that rest can be steady and allowed.[58]

LOCK IT IN:

Set a clock and sit still. No fixes, no tasks. Let your body learn that stillness is allowed. *Holding still is its own kind of strength.*

Read this when

Relationships Feel Hard

Relationships are sacred to me. You'll never hear me trash the people I've cared about, but that doesn't mean I haven't been hurt. And it doesn't mean I haven't caused hurt too. I've taken people for granted. I've let stress speak for me. I've ghosted when I didn't know how to communicate. And I've also been on the receiving end of that silence.

This section is about *the in-between...* when connection feels heavy, but not hopeless. When you're still learning how to shift energy instead of throwing fuel on a fire. When the easy thing would be to walk away, get sarcastic, shut down, or play the "they should just know" card, but you're choosing to try something different.

The coming pages are for those moments. The almost-fights. The "I didn't mean it like that." The "Why does this always happen?" They're not about perfect communication. They're about intentional pivots, when you could keep repeating the pattern... but you don't.

Grace for both sides, tools for moving forward, and reminders that showing up better is its own kind of love.

69 | Read this when *you're tired of talking but still need connection*

BURNOUT BAIT:

You don't want to be around anyone. Small talk feels unbearable. Deep talk feels impossible. You're touched out, peopled out, and worn too thin to explain what's wrong. So, you pull away, even when you're craving connection.

TACTICAL TRADE-OFF:

SIDE-BY-SIDE PRESENCE

Don't force the words. Just be near someone. Take a walk together. Watch a show. Do a task shoulder-to-shoulder. You don't have to speak to show up. Let presence carry the weight that words can't.

WHY THIS WORKS:

Shared space regulates the body even without words. Side-by-side time rebuilds connection without draining your energy.[59, 60]

LOCK IT IN:

Skip the words, share the space. Walk, work, or sit side-by-side until the air evens out. *Closeness is built in presence, not performance.*

70 | Read this when *you're distant but craving connection*

BURNOUT BAIT:

You've been pulling back. Canceling plans. Leaving texts unread. You don't want to be around anyone, but the silence is starting to get heavy. You're not upset. You're not fine either. You just feel off, and you don't know how to close the gap without making it weird.

TACTICAL TRADE-OFF:

STAY ON THE RADAR

You don't have to explain everything. Just send something honest and low-pressure:

"Haven't been in a talking mood, just didn't want to totally vanish."

or

"I've been a little off lately, don't need anything, just wanted to check in."

It's not a deep dive. It's a signal. And that's enough to shift the distance.

WHY THIS WORKS:

Stress can make closeness feel heavy, but small signals of presence retrain your system to accept connection. A simple check-in keeps distance from turning into disconnection.

LOCK IT IN:

One line is enough: "I'm off, but I'm here." Don't wait for perfect words to close the gap. *A small reach is all it takes to cut the silence.*

71 | **Read this when *your partner doesn't get it***

BURNOUT BAIT:

You start shutting down. Or snapping. Or assuming they'll never understand, so why bother explaining? They say the wrong thing or nothing at all, and it feels like one more weight to carry instead of a place to land. You're not mad they can't fix it—you're mad it feels like they don't see it.

TACTICAL TRADE-OFF:

TAKE A BREATH AND NAME WHAT YOU NEED

One deep breath. Then say it plainly, no blame, no apology. Try:

"I'm not okay, and I'm trying not to take it out on you. I just need some patience/space/connection/support right now."

or

"I'm maxed out. I don't need advice. I just need support. Or even just quiet connection."

It won't change the whole relationship in one breath, but it's a start. And starts matter.

WHY THIS WORKS:

Stress scrambles communication. Naming what you need directly gives your partner a clear way to show up and keeps resentment from building.

LOCK IT IN:

One breath. Then name what you need plain and short. Don't make them guess. ***Clarity is a bridge they can actually cross.***

72 | Read this when *you're not being fair and can't stop*

BURNOUT BAIT:

You're irritable. Impatient. Snapping at the wrong person for the wrong reason. You know it's not really about them, but you're already mid-slam, mid-sigh, mid-eye-roll. And once it starts, it's hard to stop. You're not trying to be an ass. You're just maxed out and leaking.

TACTICAL TRADE-OFF:

CALL YOURSELF OUT, OUT LOUD

Interrupt the pattern. Name it in the moment:

"That wasn't fair. I'm overwhelmed and it came out sideways."

or

"I know I'm being short; it's not you. I need a second to reset."

You're not excusing it. You're owning it. And that disrupts the spiral.

WHY THIS WORKS:

Calling yourself out breaks the spiral. Acknowledging it out loud shifts you out of defensiveness and keeps connection intact.[61]

LOCK IT IN:

Check your own trigger before you torch the room. Call it out, reset, and give grace where it's due. ***Mercy in the moment is strength under pressure.***

73 | Read this when *the people you love are getting your worst*

BURNOUT BAIT:

You held it together all shift. Stayed locked in. But by the time you walk through the door, you're cooked, and the people who love you most get the scraps. The tone. The silence. The eye-roll. You're not trying to hurt them. You're just carrying too much.

TACTICAL TRADE-OFF:

TAKE FIVE TO DUMP THE DEBRIS

Before you step inside, give yourself five minutes. Make a pitstop on the way home if you need to.

Sit in the car. Stand in the garage. Use your notes app. Voice memo it. Call a peer. Say what sucked. Vent it. Burn it.

And let your people know ahead of time:

"On my way, just need a minute to offload before I come in."

That energy has to go somewhere. Don't let it land on them.

WHY THIS WORKS:

Your system needs a buffer between the shift and home. A quick offload clears leftover stress so your family gets you, not the fall-out.[62]

LOCK IT IN:

They feel the spillover whether you admit it or not. Offload the weight before you step inside. *Home should be your refuge, not your fallout zone*

74 | Read this when *you're scared to open up*

BURNOUT BAIT:

You've seen what happens when people expose too much. You've watched trust backfire. You've learned to keep things close, control the narrative, and keep moving. Vulnerability is for later, when it's "safe. "But you keep moving the goalpost on later, and the weight keeps building.

TACTICAL TRADE-OFF:

TEST THE DOOR, DON'T BUST IT OPEN

You don't have to trauma-dump or hand over the full story. Just try one true sentence:

"Things have been heavier than I let on."

or

"I don't talk about this often, but I trust you."

or

"I'm not great at opening up, but I'm trying, and this feels like a start."

Say it to someone who's earned a little access. Not all the way open, just not locked shut.

WHY THIS WORKS:

Small, honest statements give your system proof that connection doesn't have to backfire. One controlled step builds trust without losing choice.[63]

LOCK IT IN:

You don't have to bare it all. Pick one line, one truth, and hand it over. ***Trust builds one truth at a time.***

75 | Read this when *every little thing is becoming a fight*

BURNOUT BAIT:

You snap fast. Over-explain. Get defensive before they even finish talking. Everything feels loaded. Every ask feels like pressure. And before you know it, you're mid-argument over something stupid... again.

TACTICAL TRADE-OFF:

SWITCH OUT OF FIGHT MODE

While the heat's still fresh, rewind it. What showed up in your body right before the flip? Shallow breath? Fast movements? That snap in your voice? That's your cue.

Next time it hits, *drop your shoulders and go still.* No words. No exit. Just pause. Let your body interrupt what your mouth is about to escalate.

WHY THIS WORKS:

Pausing shifts your body out of fight mode. That stillness cools activation and changes the direction of the moment before it escalates.

LOCK IT IN:

Catch the cue before your mouth takes over. Shoulders drop, breath slow, silence first. *The fight ends where your pause begins.*

76 | Read this when *you don't want to be touched*

BURNOUT BAIT:

They reach for you, and you flinch. Not because you're mad. Because you're maxed out. Your skin feels loud. Your body is on edge. Even simple touch feels like one more demand. You know they mean well, but all you want is space.

TACTICAL TRADE-OFF:

SIGNAL AND SHIFT

Say it before it builds:

"I care about you. I just need physical space right now."

or

"It's not you...I'm overstimulated. Give me a sec to reset."

Then ground yourself with firm pressure you control, hands pressing into thighs, arms crossed and squeezing your biceps, leaning into a wall or surface. Reclaim your boundary without disconnection.

WHY THIS WORKS:

Overstimulation makes touch feel like too much. Naming your need reduces confusion, and applying firm self-pressure helps your body settle without pulling away.

LOCK IT IN:

Say it straight, then ground yourself on your own terms. Boundaries don't push people out; they keep connection safe. *Clear limits protect closeness.*

77 | Read this when *you need closeness but can't ask*

BURNOUT BAIT:

You want to be close, but don't know how to say it. You're not mad, but you're distant. You're not okay, but you're quiet. You hope they'll notice, but you can't bring yourself to ask. It feels too exposed. Too vulnerable. Too much. So, you act fine and feel worse.

TACTICAL TRADE-OFF:

OPEN THE DOOR...JUST A LITTLE

Don't overexplain. Don't armor up. Try something simple but honest:

"I'm not great at asking, but I could use a little closeness."

or

"Can we just sit together? No talking, I just don't want to be alone right now."

It's not about fixing anything. It's about being near what softens you.

WHY THIS WORKS:

Stress can make connection feel risky, but small honest asks give your system a way back in. Simple signals rebuild closeness without forcing it.

LOCK IT IN:

You don't need to explain the ache, just name the need. A simple ask opens the door. *Courage is often just one honest sentence spoken out loud.*

RELATIONSHIPS

78 | Read this when *something feels off between you*

BURNOUT BAIT:

Nothing's wrong, but it's not right either. You're going through the motions. Conversations feel surface-level. Physical closeness feels routine. You're there, but not really with them, and you can't put your finger on what changed. So, you stay quiet and hope it shifts on its own.

TACTICAL TRADE-OFF:

NAME THE FOG, NOT THE FIX

You don't need a solution. Just say what's true:

"Something feels off between us. I don't know what it is, but I miss feeling close."

or

"I've felt disconnected lately. I don't think it's just you, but I didn't want to keep pretending I was fine."

Saying it out loud brings both of you into the same space, even if the clarity comes later.

WHY THIS WORKS:

Disconnection grows in silence. Shedding light on it without blame brings awareness back and creates space for real closeness to return.[64]

LOCK IT IN:

Don't ignore the undercurrent, the quiet shift you both feel but won't name. You don't need the fix yet, just the truth. *Honesty is the compass that points you back together.*

Read this when you're
Questioning Everything

The night I arrested a 74-year-old woman with dementia still gnaws at me. She had pulled a knife on her husband, the danger was real, but cuffing her felt wrong in my bones. I pushed back. I questioned it. I tried every angle I could think of to find another way. My supervisor shut me down. The prosecutor doubled down. By the time it was over, she was in the back of my cruiser, and I was sick to my stomach.

That's how moral injury works its way in. You know what feels right, but the system corners you into something else. You do the job because you have to, and later you're left replaying it, wondering what it cost, wondering what else you'll be asked to swallow.

These entries are for those moments. When orders collide with values. When doing the job leaves you questioning yourself long after the call ends. What follows isn't about easy answers, it's re-anchoring in what you know to be true, checking your lens, and finding a way to stand steady in yourself when everything around you feels off-center.

79 | Read this when *you feel like the job is breaking you*

BURNOUT BAIT:

You swallow it. You tell yourself to just keep grinding, that breaking is part of the deal, and you let the weight stack higher until numbness feels like the only shield.

TACTICAL TRADE-OFF:

FLIP THE FRAME

Ask yourself: *"What is this building in me?"* Then scan your body for the cue, tight jaw, shallow breath, clenched fists. Release one of them on purpose. Give your body the signal that you're not breaking, you're resetting.

WHY THIS WORKS:

Reframing shifts the story from collapse to choice. Pairing it with a physical release tells your body it's not stuck and helps stop the burnout loop.

LOCK IT IN:

Flip the frame. The strain isn't breaking you; it's shaping you. Release the tension and claim the reset. *You're not breaking, you're being forged stronger.*

DOUBT

80 | Read this when *you wonder if you're still good at this*

BURNOUT BAIT:

You spiral into comparison, measuring yourself against old versions of you or against others who look like they're holding it together better. You let doubt pile on top of fatigue until you convince yourself you've lost it.

TACTICAL TRADE-OFF:

CHECK THE EVIDENCE

Instead of replaying the worst calls in your head, name three things you did well today, even if they feel small. Write them down, say them out loud, or text them to someone you trust. Put proof back in front of your own eyes.

WHY THIS WORKS:

Self-doubt filters out your wins. Calling out a few real examples puts proof back in view and strengthens confidence.[65]

LOCK IT IN:

Doubt feeds on selective memory. Call up what you've actually done, not the ghosts of what you fear you've missed. *Your capability doesn't vanish, it's always there to claim.*

DOUBT

81 | **Read this when *you feel like you failed someone***

BURNOUT BAIT:

You hang on to the guilt, even when no one else is asking you to. You replay it, punish yourself with it, and call it accountability, when really, it's self-destruction.

TACTICAL TRADE-OFF:

PRACTICE SELF-FORGIVENESS

Say it out loud, clear and deliberate:

I failed in that moment.
Failure is part of life.
It does not erase my worth.
It does not erase my intent.

Breathe it in. Forgiveness isn't forgetting, it's release. It's the act of refusing to bleed forever from one cut.

WHY THIS WORKS:

Without forgiveness, guilt hardens into shame. Owning the failure, then releasing it, keeps the lesson while stopping the self-punishment.[66]

LOCK IT IN:

Failure happens, but dragging it forever is a choice. Own it, breathe it, then release it. *Accountability means learning the lesson, not living in the wound.*

DOUBT

82 | Read this when *you think you have to suffer to grow*

BURNOUT BAIT:

You stay in the trenches longer than you need to, convinced that grinding yourself down is the only way to build toughness. You collect scars as proof of strength, even when the scars cost you more than they give back.

TACTICAL TRADE-OFF:

CHOOSE YOUR CHALLENGE

Pain will find you, life guarantees that. But strength doesn't come from stacking unnecessary suffering. It comes from the challenges you step into on purpose. The next time you catch yourself defaulting to "more hurt = more strong," redirect. Do something that trains you instead of drains you:

- hit a workout
- run drills
- pick up a book that stretches your thinking
- call someone who sharpens you.

Build capacity with intention, not punishment.

WHY THIS WORKS:

Growth comes from stress paired with recovery, not endless strain. Choosing intentional challenges builds real capacity without needless damage.[67]

LOCK IT IN:

Stop mistaking punishment for progress. You don't need extra scars to prove strength. *Growth is forged by deliberate fire, not random flames.*

83 | **Read this when *your faith in the system is gone***

BURNOUT BAIT:

You stew in it. You let bitterness set up shop, replaying every broken promise and every leader who looked the other way. Cynicism becomes the only lens you see through, and it drains you faster than the job itself.

TACTICAL TRADE-OFF:

ANCHOR TO THE MISSION

If the system feels cracked, narrow your focus to the one thing that still holds: the person in front of you. The call, the victim, the family, or your team. Redirect your energy from the failed structure to the human mission right in front of you.

WHY THIS WORKS:

Focusing on the human mission restores meaning when the larger system feels broken. It protects your integrity and keeps cynicism from taking over.[68]

LOCK IT IN:

When the structure cracks, zoom in tighter, the person, the moment, or the ground right under your boots. *Purpose holds when politics fail.*

84 | Read this when *you feel betrayed*

BURNOUT BAIT:

You let the betrayal take the wheel. Replay it. Obsess over the lie, the politics, the person who sold you out. Anger hardens into cynicism, and now you're carrying their dishonor like it belongs to you.

TACTICAL TRADE-OFF:

DRAW THE LINE

Betrayal blurs the edges between *their failure* and *your worth*. Grab a page and split it down the middle. On the left: what they did. On the right: who you still are, your values, your standards, your mission. Then destroy the left side. Rip it, burn it, shred it, whatever makes it clear that their failure is not yours to hold. Keep the right side where you'll see it again.

WHY THIS WORKS:

Betrayal makes it easy to confuse their actions with your value. Writing it down and tearing up their side makes it clear: their choices are theirs, and your integrity is still yours.[69]

LOCK IT IN:

Betrayal stings because it hits where trust once lived. Let their choice stay with them, not in you. *Your integrity is the ground they can't take from you.*

DOUBT

85 | Read this when *you're "why" feels out of reach*

BURNOUT BAIT:

You chase the big answer in circles, demanding to know the "why" all at once. When it doesn't come, you sink into frustration or emptiness, convinced your purpose has disappeared.

TACTICAL TRADE-OFF:

ZOOM IN

Forget the lifelong map. Ask instead: *What's the next right move?* Anchor to one choice today that lines up with your values, whether it's showing up, listening, protecting, or learning. Purpose doesn't vanish. It's built in the small, repeated steps.

WHY THIS WORKS:

Purpose isn't a single answer. Focusing on small choices that match your values lowers pressure and builds meaning over time.

LOCK IT IN:

Stop chasing the grand answer. Anchor to one choice today that reflects who you are. *Meaning is built in the small moves repeated.*

DOUBT

86 | **Read this when *you don't recognize yourself anymore***

BURNOUT BAIT:

You avoid the mirror. You bury yourself in the grind, convincing yourself that disappearing into the work is easier than facing the version of you that feels unrecognizable.

TACTICAL TRADE-OFF:

TRACE THE THREAD

Pick one thing that's always been yours... your humor, your grit, your love for your people, your curiosity, your faith. Name it. Touch it. Let that thread remind you that even if parts of you feel hidden under the weight, your core hasn't vanished.

WHY THIS WORKS:

Burnout can blur your sense of self. Reconnecting with one core trait or value restores continuity and reminds you your foundation is still intact.

LOCK IT IN:

Stress can bury parts of you, but it can't erase them. Grab the thread you still trust and pull it forward. *The core of you is steady and it's waiting for you to stand in it again.*

DOUBT

87 | Read this when *"I'm fine" feels like a lie*

BURNOUT BAIT:

You double down on the mask. You keep saying it *"I'm fine"* because it feels safer than letting anyone see the cracks. Meanwhile, the pressure builds behind closed doors until it spills out sideways.

TACTICAL TRADE-OFF:

DROP ONE LAYER

You don't have to unload everything. Choose one small truth you can admit, to yourself, to a journal, to a trusted peer. *"I'm exhausted." "That call shook me." "I don't have it all together today."* One layer dropped keeps the dam from bursting.

WHY THIS WORKS:

Revealing even one small truth reduces the hidden load. It breaks isolation and makes space for authenticity without needing a full unload.[70, 71]

LOCK IT IN:

Every mask has a weight. Drop one layer, even a small truth, and breathe lighter. ***Freedom starts the second you stop performing.***

DOUBT

88 | Read this when *you forgot who you are without the badge*

BURNOUT BAIT:

You fuse your whole identity to the uniform. You tell yourself that without the badge, you're nothing, and that belief keeps you trapped, overworking to prove your worth.

TACTICAL TRADE-OFF:

NAME WHAT'S BEYOND

List three parts of you that existed before the job, or that would still exist if the job ended tomorrow. Father. Mother. Friend. Athlete. Builder. Creator. Anchor to the truth that the badge is what you do, not who you are.

WHY THIS WORKS:

Tying your worth only to the job makes you fragile when the role shifts. Remembering the parts of you that exist beyond the badge keeps your identity steady.[72]

LOCK IT IN:

The badge is a role, not your soul. Name what existed before it and what will remain after. *It isn't an issued accessory; it's the foundation you stand on.*

DOUBT

Read this when
You Need to Debrief Together

For a long time, I suffered alone. I healed alone, in the grind for years. I thought that was enough, just push through, figure it out, keep moving. But here's what I learned: the biggest accelerator in my healing and growth wasn't grinding it out, it was opening up. Not pushing against, but letting go. The minute I let someone else in, the weight shifted. That's when I started to feel real support, real relief, and the freedom to finally breathe a different kind of breath.

And here's the reality: the number one factor in how well you recover after a critical incident isn't what happens after it, it's the support system you already have in place before it ever goes down.[73] The relationships you build now are the ones that steady you when it hits.

That's peer-to-peer offload. Tactical co-regulation. Real-time repair. It doesn't have to be complicated. Sometimes it's a quick exchange in passing, sometimes it's taking a few minutes at the end of shift.

These tactics will help you build that net before you need it. To make connection a deliberate part of the job, the same way gear and training are. These entries give you ways to debrief together in real time, so the weight doesn't linger where it doesn't belong.

89 | Read this when *the call landed heavy on both of you*

BURNOUT BAIT:

Stay silent, swallow it, and hope it fades on its own. You tell yourself it's "part of the job" and pretend it didn't register. But it lingers, between you, in you, and hardens into the kind of weight that doesn't move unless spoken.

TACTICAL TRADE-OFF:

PASS THE MIC DRILL

Take turns saying one sentence each about what hit you. No long stories, no over-explaining. Just short hits: "That one shook me." "It reminded me of..." "I can't get the sound out of my head." Pass it back and forth until the edge softens, then close it with one line each about what you need next: "I'm good to move on," or "Can we check back later?"

WHY THIS WORKS:

Speaking short lines turns the weight into language your system can process. It stops the loop from running silent and gives closure with a clear next step.[74]

LOCK IT IN:

Don't leave the silence to calcify. Pass the weight back and forth, piece by piece. *Shared words cut the load in half.*

90 | Read this when *you don't know what to say after what you saw*

BURNOUT BAIT:

Shut down. Numb out. Pretend the images aren't replaying in your mind and wait for them to fade. But silence doesn't erase them, it just locks them in deeper.

TACTICAL TRADE-OFF:

SHARED SILENCE RESET

If words won't come, agree to a minute or two of steady breathing side by side. No pressure to talk, just presence. Set your eyes on the same fixed point (dashboard light, wall spot, horizon). When it feels right, one of you can break the silence with a simple opener: "Want to say anything?" or "You good to leave it here?" That way, space is given, but the choice stays open.

WHY THIS WORKS:

Shared silence helps both systems settle together. Adding a simple opening leaves room for words without demand.[75]

LOCK IT IN:

Silence doesn't mean absence, it means you're holding space. Share the air first, the words will follow. *Steadiness speaks before language does.*

DEBRIEF

91 | Read this when *you need to talk, but can't find the words*

BURNOUT BAIT:

Keep it bottled. Wait until you can line up the perfect words in your head, or worse, convince yourself it's not worth saying at all. The weight only grows heavier when left unspoken.

TACTICAL TRADE-OFF:

TRADE THE FRAGMENTS

Neither of you needs a full story. Each of you puts one short fragment on the table, "That sucked," "Can't shake the look on their face," "I feel off." Go back and forth a couple of times. It's not a conversation; it's a shared unload. The point is, nobody holds it alone.

WHY THIS WORKS:

Even fragmented words move the weight out of your head. Getting it out shifts the brain from raw sensation into language and lowers the intensity.[76]

LOCK IT IN:

You don't need perfect speech. Get it out raw, crooked, messy. One offloads, the other catches. *Unspoken pressure grows heavy, even jagged words cut it loose.*

DEBRIEF

92 | **Read this when *your partner goes quiet after the call***

BURNOUT BAIT:

Poke, prod, or push. Demand they talk right now because you don't like the quiet. But forcing words only drives them further inside.

TACTICAL TRADE-OFF:

ANCHOR WITHOUT ASKING

Skip the interrogation. Sit in the same space, steady your presence, and sync one small action, both pour water, both take off boots, both sit in stillness. A simple line is enough: "I'm here when you want." Then let the quiet hold until one leans in.

WHY THIS WORKS:

Staying present without forcing words gives their system space to reset. Calm signals show they can re-engage on their own terms.

LOCK IT IN:

You don't need to crack each other open. Just hold steady in the same space until the quiet softens. *Stability is shown in the silence you're willing to share.*

DEBRIEF

93 | **Read this when** *the silence between you is getting loud*

BURNOUT BAIT:

Keep pretending it's fine. Let the gap stretch until the silence feels heavier than words ever would. That distance breeds resentment instead of relief.

TACTICAL TRADE-OFF:

BREAK THE STATIC

Cut the tension and do something small together. Grab coffee, knock out a quick task, or throw a dry joke across the room. The point isn't deep talk; it's clearing the air together so connection can slip back in.

WHY THIS WORKS:

A small spark, humor, action, or a light ask, shifts both systems out of shutdown. It breaks the loop and makes space for real connection.[77]

LOCK IT IN:

Prolonged silence isn't neutral; it grows teeth the longer you leave it. Break it as a team with something small. *Even a crack in the quiet lets connection back in.*

94 | Read this when *the call makes you both short-tempered with each other*

BURNOUT BAIT:

Snap at each other. Nitpick the smallest thing, the way they drove, the way you logged the run, the way they looked at you. Let the spillover from the call turn into a fight you don't even mean.

TACTICAL TRADE-OFF:

FLAG IT

Before it escalates, throw a flag: "This isn't about you, that was the call talking." It's not an apology tour, just a reset button. Follow it with a small redirect, "Give me a second," or "Let's shake it off." A quick acknowledgment plus a shift in focus stops the bleed-over before it turns personal.

WHY THIS WORKS:

Irritability after a call is spillover, not a reflection of the relationship. Calling it out for what it is creates separation and stops it from turning into a fight.[78]

LOCK IT IN:

Snapping at each other isn't about the call, it's about what it left behind. Say it out loud before it sets the two of you against each other. *Don't let the job turn teammates into targets.*

DEBRIEF

95 | Read this when *the dark humor is hitting harder than it's helping*

BURNOUT BAIT:

Keep doubling down on the jokes. Laugh louder, push the sarcasm further, and hope the sting goes away. But the punchlines land flat, and what was meant to lighten the mood just deepens the heaviness.

TACTICAL TRADE-OFF:

SWITCH THE CHANNEL

Call it when the jokes turn heavy: "Too dark." Then swap cheesy one-liners back and forth, knock-knocks, dad jokes, the corniest stuff you can dig up. Take turns until the laugh feels lighter.

WHY THIS WORKS:

Dark humor vents pressure but can leave residue. Pivoting together into silly humor resets the release and gives your systems a clean break.

LOCK IT IN:

When the dark gets heavy, call it and swap the script. Cheesy back-and-forth turns relief into real reset. *Laughter is a tool; don't let it turn into another wound.*

DEBRIEF

96 | **Read this when** *one of you hides in busywork instead of talking*

BURNOUT BAIT:

Let them bury themselves in wiping down tools, stacking papers, scrolling reports. You tell yourself it's fine, they're "just keeping busy." Meanwhile the weight of the call doesn't go anywhere, it just settles deeper.

TACTICAL TRADE-OFF:

INTERRUPT THE ROUTINE

Step into the task with them, grab the rag, stack the papers, stand shoulder-to-shoulder. While you're both moving, drop one honest line: "That one was rough." Shared motion plus a shared word turns avoidance into connection.

WHY THIS WORKS:

Avoidance keeps stress locked in. Pairing light action with a small acknowledgment gives the nervous system both movement and release, lowering the pressure without forcing a sit-down talk.

LOCK IT IN:

Busy hands can be a shield, but shields don't lighten the load. Step into motion together and let the truth come out. *Motion shared is weight reduced.*

97 | Read this when *one of you needs words and other doesn't*

BURNOUT BAIT:

Dig your heels in. Either unload every detail until they shut down, or cut them off with "I'm over it" and leave them hanging. Both paths widen the gap instead of closing it.

TACTICAL TRADE-OFF:

SET THE SPLIT SCREEN

Name it openly: "I need to talk this out," or "I need to let this one go." Then agree on the lane: one vents for a set time while the other holds space, or you both circle back later. Each gets what they need because both agree. The goal isn't perfect balance; it's clarity that prevents resentment.

WHY THIS WORKS:

Conflicting debrief styles are normal. Naming what you each need creates structure, which calms the nervous system and lowers frustration on both sides.

LOCK IT IN:

Not every debrief looks the same. One of you needs words, the other needs quiet, both are valid. ***Respect the lane, and you'll both get where you need to go.***

DEBRIEF

98 | Read this when *one of you is wired and the other is wiped out*

BURNOUT BAIT:

Force each other into your lane. Try to hype up the one who's drained, or shut down the one who's buzzing. Both backfires, you end up frustrated and more disconnected.

TACTICAL TRADE-OFF:

CALL IT, THEN COVER

Say it straight: "You're still running hot, I'm crashing." Then treat it like a handoff: "You take the edge right now; I'll regroup and cover later." By naming the contrast and sharing the load, you turn mismatch into teamwork instead of conflict.

WHY THIS WORKS:

Energy mismatches are biology, not personal flaws. Calling it out reduces friction, and framing it as a relay builds trust that you've got each other's backs even when you're not in sync.

LOCK IT IN:

You won't always be on the same rhythm. Be open and direct in the sharing and the receiving, then trade the edge when it's time. *Flex as a unit, the strongest partnerships bend so they don't break.*

99 | Read this when *the call keeps bleeding into the next*

BURNOUT BAIT:

Charge straight into the next run without a pause. Pretend the weight isn't still on your back. But when you carry one scene into the next, it piles up fast, and neither of you gets a clean slate.

TACTICAL TRADE-OFF:

MARK THE RESET

Do a reset ritual together before rolling out, tap the dash, fist bump, say "Clear." Doesn't matter what it is, only that it's shared. It signals to both brains: that call is closed, we step into the next one fresh.

WHY THIS WORKS:

Transitions matter. A physical or verbal marker cues the nervous system to close one loop before opening the next, which lowers carryover stress and keeps the build-up from stacking shift after shift.[79]

LOCK IT IN:

You won't erase the call, and you're not meant to. What matters is closing it together, and if the debris stays, revisit it on your terms. Then step into the next call with your full strength of who you are.

ENDNOTES

1   Jill Bolte Taylor. (2016). *My stroke of insight: A Brain Scientist's Personal Journey*. Penguin Books.

2   Pillay, S. (2017, May 4). *Secret to brain success: Intelligent cognitive rest*. Harvard Health Blog. https://www.health.harvard.edu/blog/secret-to-brain-success-intelligent-cognitive-rest-2017050411705

3   Lu, W.-A., Chen, G.-Y., & Kuo, C.-D. (2011). Foot reflexology can increase vagal modulation, decrease sympathetic modulation, and lower blood pressure in healthy subjects and patients with coronary artery disease. *Alternative Therapies in Health and Medicine*, 17(4), 8–14. https://pubmed.ncbi.nlm.nih.gov/22314629/

4   Toussaint, L., Nguyen, Q. A., Roettger, C., Dixon, K., Offenbächer, M., Kohls, N., Hirsch, J., & Sirois, F. (2021). Effectiveness of Progressive Muscle Relaxation, Deep Breathing, and Guided Imagery in Promoting Psychological and Physiological States of Relaxation. *Evidence-Based Complementary and Alternative Medicine*, 2021(1), 1–8. https://doi.org/10.1155/2021/5924040

5   Wadji, D. L., Martin-Soelch, C., & Camos, V. (2022). Can working memory account for EMDR efficacy in PTSD? *BMC Psychology*, 10(1). https://doi.org/10.1186/s40359-022-00951-0

6   Basso, J. C., & Suzuki, W. A. (2017). The Effects of Acute Exercise on Mood, Cognition, Neurophysiology, and Neurochemical Pathways: a Review. *Brain Plasticity*, 2(2), 127–152. https://doi.org/10.3233/bpl-160040

7   Bach, D., Groesbeck, G., Stapleton, P., Sims, R., Blickheuser, K., & Church, D. (2019). Clinical EFT (Emotional Freedom Techniques) improves multiple physiological markers of health. *Journal of Evidence-Based Integrative Medicine*, 24, 2515690X18823691. https://doi.org/10.1177/2515690X18823691

8   Reynolds, S., Lane, S. J., & Mullen, B. (2015). Effects of Deep Pressure Stimulation on Physiological Arousal. *American Journal of Occupational Therapy*, 69(3), 6903350010p1. https://doi.org/10.5014/ajot.2015.015560

9   Khir, S. M., Yunus, W. M. A. W. M., Mahmud, N., Wang, R., Panatik, S. A., Sukor, M. S. M., & Nordin, N. A. (2024). Efficacy of Progressive Muscle Relaxation in Adults for Stress, Anxiety, and Depression: A Systematic Review. *Psychology Research and Behavior Management*, 17(1), 345–365. https://doi.org/10.2147/PRBM.S437277

10 Toussaint, L., Nguyen, Q. A., Roettger, C., Dixon, K., Offenbächer, M., Kohls, N., Hirsch, J., & Sirois, F. (2021). Effectiveness of Progressive Muscle Relaxation, Deep Breathing, and Guided Imagery in Promoting Psychological and Physiological States of Relaxation. *Evidence-Based Complementary and Alternative Medicine*, 2021(1), 1–8. https://doi.org/10.1155/2021/5924040

11 Balban, M. Y., Neri, E., Kogon, M. M., Weed, L., Nouriani, B., Jo, B., Holl, G., Zeitzer, J. M., Spiegel, D., & Huberman, A. D. (2023). Brief structured respiration practices enhance mood and reduce physiological arousal. *Cell Reports Medicine*, 4(1), 1–15. https://doi.org/10.1016/j.xcrm.2022.100895

12 Hogendoorn, H., Kammers, M., Haggard, P., & Verstraten, F. (2015). Self-touch modulates the somatosensory evoked P100. *Experimental Brain Research*, 233(10), 2845–2858. https://doi.org/10.1007/s00221-015-4355-0

13 Payne, P., Levine, P. A., & Crane-Godreau, M. A. (2015). Somatic experiencing: Using interoception and proprioception as core elements of trauma therapy. *Frontiers in Psychology*, 6(93), 1–18. https://doi.org/10.3389/fpsyg.2015.00093

14 Kramer, C. K., & Cristiane Bauermann Leitao. (2023). Laughter as medicine: A systematic review and meta-analysis of interventional studies evaluating the impact of spontaneous laughter on cortisol levels. *PLoS One*, 18(5), e0286260–e0286260. https://doi.org/10.1371/journal.pone.0286260

15 Jones, C. A. (2025, June 9). *Research shows bilateral stimulation calms the amygdala | Bi-Tapp*. Bi-Tapp.com. https://bi-tapp.com/bilateral-stimulation-is-a-self-regulation-resource/

16 Kramer, C. K., & Cristiane Bauermann Leitao. (2023). Laughter as medicine: A systematic review and meta-analysis of interventional studies evaluating the impact of spontaneous laughter on cortisol levels. *PLoS One*, 18(5), e0286260–e0286260. https://doi.org/10.1371/journal.pone.0286260

17 Khir, S. M., Yunus, W. M. A. W. M., Mahmud, N., Wang, R., Panatik, S. A., Sukor, M. S. M., & Nordin, N. A. (2024). Efficacy of Progressive Muscle Relaxation in Adults for Stress, Anxiety, and Depression: A Systematic Review. *Psychology Research and Behavior Management*, 17(1), 345–365. https://doi.org/10.2147/PRBM.S437277

18 Balban, M. Y., Neri, E., Kogon, M. M., Weed, L., Nouriani, B., Jo, B., Holl, G., Zeitzer, J. M., Spiegel, D., & Huberman, A. D. (2023). Brief structured respiration practices enhance mood and reduce physiological arousal. *Cell Reports Medicine*, 4(1), 1–15. https://doi.org/10.1016/j.xcrm.2022.100895

19 https://pmc.ncbi.nlm.nih.gov/articles/PMC9305111/pdf/NYAS-1510-68.pdf

20 Thaut, M. H., McIntosh, G. C., & Hoemberg, V. (2015). Neurobiological foundations of neurologic music therapy: rhythmic entrainment and the motor system. *Frontiers in Psychology*, 5(1185). https://doi.org/10.3389/fpsyg.2014.01185

21 Gallo, I. S., Keil, A., McClure, S. M., & Rocklage, M. (2014). The cognitive neuroscience of emotion regulation: From regulation strategies to neurophysiological processes. *Frontiers in Psychology*, 5, Article 1185. https://doi.org/10.3389/fpsyg.2014.01185

22 Lamson, N., & Meissner, C. A. (2020). How the confirmation bias influences interrogators' evaluations of suspects: Evidence from a novel experimental paradigm. *Journal of Visualized Experiments*, 2020(155), e60620. https://doi.org/10.3791/60620

23 Suda, M., Sugimura, K., & Kawashima, R. (2022). Active touch and somatosensory perception: Influence of attention-dependent mechanisms. *Frontiers in Integrative Neuroscience*, 16, 871227. https://doi.org/10.3389/fnint.2022.871227

24 Schmid, P. C., Kleiman, T., Amodio, D. M., & Cresswell, J. D. (2021). Neural mechanisms of emotion regulation: A review of fMRI studies on reappraisal and mindfulness-based strategies. *Frontiers in Psychology*, 12, 621958. https://doi.org/10.3389/fpsyg.2021.621958

25 Johnson-Glenberg, M. C., & Megowan-Romanowicz, C. (2017). Embodied science and mixed reality: How gesture and motion capture affect physics education. *Cognitive Research: Principles and Implications*, 2(1). https://doi.org/10.1186/s41235-017-0060-9

26 Rosen, G. M. (2023). Revisiting the Origins of EMDR. *Journal of Contemporary Psychotherapy*, 53(53). https://doi.org/10.1007/s10879-023-09582-x

27 Korhonen, M., Komulainen, K., & Okkonen, V. (2020). Burnout as an identity rupture in the life course: a longitudinal narrative method. *Sociology of Health & Illness*, 42(8), 1918–1933. https://doi.org/10.1111/1467-9566.13183

28 Tiia Kekäläinen, Luchetti, M., Terracciano, A., Gamaldo, A. A., Mogle, J., Lovett, H. H., Brown, J., Timo Rantalainen, Sliwinski, M. J., & Sutin, A. R. (2023). Physical activity and cognitive function: moment-to-moment and day-to-day associations. *International Journal of Behavioral Nutrition and Physical Activity*, 20(1). https://doi.org/10.1186/s12966-023-01536-9

29 Sumitra, L., & Aniruddha, G. (2025). Hydration Status and Its Impact on Cognitive Performance and Reaction Time in Young Adults: A Comparative Study. *International Journal of Academic Medicine and Pharmacy*, 7 (2); 157-162. https://www.academicmed.org/Uploads/Volume7Issue2/33.%20[4805.%20JAMP_Mohamed]%20157-162.pdf

30   Tiia Kekäläinen, Luchetti, M., Terracciano, A., Gamaldo, A. A., Mogle, J., Lovett, H. H., Brown, J., Timo Rantalainen, Sliwinski, M. J., & Sutin, A. R. (2023). Physical activity and cognitive function: moment-to-moment and day-to-day associations. *International Journal of Behavioral Nutrition and Physical Activity*, 20(1). https://doi.org/10.1186/s12966-023-01536-9

31   Donovan, N. (2022). Peer support facilitates post-traumatic growth in first responders: A literature review. *Trauma*, 24(4), 146040862210794. https://doi.org/10.1177/14604086221079441

32   Patricia Demierre Berberat. (2023). The Benefits of Grounding Strategies in Emotion and Arousal Regulation. *Mental Health & Human Resilience International Journal*, 7(2), 1–6. https://doi. org/10.23880/mhrij-16000233

33   Jiang, J., Borowiak, K., Tudge, L., Otto, C., & von Kriegstein, K. (2016). Neural mechanisms of eye contact when listening to another person talking. *Social Cognitive and Affective Neuroscience*, 12(2). https://doi. org/10.1093/scan/nsw127

34   Bach, D., Groesbeck, G., Stapleton, P., Sims, R., Blickheuser, K., & Church, D. (2019). Clinical EFT (Emotional Freedom Techniques) improves multiple physiological markers of health. *Journal of Evidence-Based Integrative Medicine*, 24, 2515690X18823691. https://doi. org/10.1177/2515690X18823691

35   Vojtova, H., & Hasto, J. (2009). Neurobiology of Eye Movement Desensitization and Reprocessing. *Activitas Nervosa Superior*, 51(3), 98–102. https://doi.org/10.1007/bf03379925

36   Tod, D., Hardy, J., & Oliver, E. (2011). Effects of Self-Talk: A Systematic Review. *Journal of Sport and Exercise Psychology*, 33(5), 666–687. https://doi.org/10.1123/jsep.33.5.666

37   Albulescu, P., Macsinga, I., Rusu, A., Sulea, C., Bodnaru, A., & Tulbure, B. T. (2022). "Give Me a Break!" a Systematic Review and meta-analysis on the Efficacy of micro-breaks for Increasing well-being and Performance. *PLoS One*, 17(8). https://doi.org/10.1371/journal. pone.0272460

38   *Acupressure for Nausea and Vomiting*. (2019). Memorial Sloan Kettering Cancer Center. https://www.mskcc.org/cancer-care/patient-education/acupressure-nausea-and-vomiting

39   Gazerani, P. (2025). The neuroplastic brain: current breakthroughs and emerging frontiers. *Brain Research*, 1858, 149643. https://doi. org/10.1016/j.brainres.2025.149643

40   Lieberman, M. D., Eisenberger, N. I., Crockett, M. J., Tom, S. M., Pfeifer, J. H., & Way, B. M. (2007). Putting feelings into words: affect labeling disrupts amygdala activity in response to affective stimuli. *Psychological Science*, 18(5), 421–428. https://doi.org/10.1111/j.1467-9280.2007.01916.x

41 Rollwage, M., Loosen, A., Hauser, T. U., Moran, R., Dolan, R. J., & Fleming, S. M. (2020). Confidence Drives a Neural Confirmation Bias. *Nature Communications*, 11(1). https://doi.org/10.1038/s41467-020-16278-6

42 Rollwage, M., Loosen, A., Hauser, T. U., Moran, R., Dolan, R. J., & Fleming, S. M. (2020). Confidence Drives a Neural Confirmation Bias. *Nature Communications*, 11(1). https://doi.org/10.1038/s41467-020-16278-6

43 *Personality and Social Psychology Review* 1 -25. (n.d.). https://faculty.haas.berkeley.edu/jschroeder/Publications/Hobson%20et%20al%20Psychology%20of%20Rituals.pdf?

44 Bach, D., Groesbeck, G., Stapleton, P., Sims, R., Blickheuser, K., & Church, D. (2019). Clinical EFT (Emotional Freedom Techniques) improves multiple physiological markers of health. *Journal of Evidence-Based Integrative Medicine*, 24, 2515690X18823691. https://doi.org/10.1177/2515690X18823691

45 Balban, M. Y., Neri, E., Kogon, M. M., Weed, L., Nouriani, B., Jo, B., Holl, G., Zeitzer, J. M., Spiegel, D., & Huberman, A. D. (2023). Brief structured respiration practices enhance mood and reduce physiological arousal. *Cell Reports Medicine*, 4(1), 1–15. https://doi.org/10.1016/j.xcrm.2022.100895

46 Payne, P., Levine, P. A., & Crane-Godreau, M. A. (2015). Somatic experiencing: Using interoception and proprioception as core elements of trauma therapy. *Frontiers in Psychology*, 6(93), 1–18. https://doi.org/10.3389/fpsyg.2015.00093

47 Levine, P. A. (1997). *Waking the Tiger: Healing Trauma*. Berkeley, CA: North Atlantic Books.

48 McGlone, F., Kerstin Uvnäs Moberg, Henrik Norholt, Eggart, M., & Müller-Oerlinghausen, B. (2024). Touch medicine: bridging the gap between recent insights from touch research and clinical medicine and its special significance for the treatment of affective disorders. *Frontiers in Psychiatry*, 15. https://doi.org/10.3389/fpsyt.2024.1390673

49 Bach, D., Groesbeck, G., Stapleton, P., Sims, R., Blickheuser, K., & Church, D. (2019). Clinical EFT (Emotional Freedom Techniques) improves multiple physiological markers of health. *Journal of Evidence-Based Integrative Medicine*, 24, 2515690X18823691. https://doi.org/10.1177/2515690X18823691

50 Cleare, S., Gumley, A., & O'Connor, R. C. (2019). Self-compassion, Self-forgiveness, Suicidal ideation and Self-harm: a Systematic review. *Clinical Psychology & Psychotherapy*, 26(5). https://doi.org/10.1002/cpp.2372

51 Balban, M. Y., Neri, E., Kogon, M. M., Weed, L., Nouriani, B., Jo, B., Holl, G., Zeitzer, J. M., Spiegel, D., & Huberman, A. D. (2023). Brief structured respiration practices enhance mood and reduce physiological arousal. *Cell Reports Medicine*, 4(1), 1–15. https://doi.org/10.1016/j.xcrm.2022.100895

52 Levine, P. A. (1997). *Waking the Tiger: Healing Trauma*. Berkeley, CA: North Atlantic Books.

53 Levine, P. A. (1997). *Waking the Tiger: Healing Trauma*. Berkeley, CA: North Atlantic Books.

54 *Personality and Social Psychology Review* 1 -25. (n.d.). https://faculty.haas.berkeley.edu/jschroeder/Publications/Hobson%20et%20al%20Psychology%20of%20Rituals.pdf?

55 *Personality and Social Psychology Review* 1 -25. (n.d.). https://faculty.haas.berkeley.edu/jschroeder/Publications/Hobson%20et%20al%20Psychology%20of%20Rituals.pdf?

56 Glass, O., Dreusicke, M., Evans, J., Bechard, E., & Wolever, R. Q. (2019). Expressive writing to improve resilience to trauma: A clinical feasibility trial. *Complementary Therapies in Clinical Practice*, 34(1), 240–246. https://doi.org/10.1016/j.ctcp.2018.12.005

57 Porges, S. W. (2025). Polyvagal Theory: Current Status, Clinical Applications, and Future Directions. *PubMed*, 22(3), 169–184. https://doi.org/10.36131/cnfioritieditore20250301

58 *Personality and Social Psychology Review* 1 -25. (n.d.). https://faculty.haas.berkeley.edu/jschroeder/Publications/Hobson%20et%20al%20Psychology%20of%20Rituals.pdf?

59 Kramer, C. K., & Cristiane Bauermann Leitao. (2023). Laughter as medicine: A systematic review and meta-analysis of interventional studies evaluating the impact of spontaneous laughter on cortisol levels. *PLoS One*, 18(5), e0286260–e0286260. https://doi.org/10.1371/journal.pone.0286260

60 Donovan, N. (2022). Peer support facilitates post-traumatic growth in first responders: A literature review. *Trauma*, 24(4), 146040862210794. https://doi.org/10.1177/14604086221079441

61 Rizkalla, L., Wertheim, E. H., & Hodgson, L. K. (2008). The roles of emotion management and perspective taking in individuals' conflict management styles and disposition to forgive. *Journal of Research in Personality*, 42(6), 1594–1601. https://doi.org/10.1016/j.jrp.2008.07.014

62 Kramer, C. K., & Cristiane Bauermann Leitao. (2023). Laughter as medicine: A systematic review and meta-analysis of interventional studies evaluating the impact of spontaneous laughter on cortisol levels. *PLoS One*, 18(5), e0286260–e0286260. https://doi.org/10.1371/journal.pone.0286260

63 Donovan, N. (2022). Peer support facilitates post-traumatic growth in first responders: A literature review. *Trauma*, 24(4), 146040862210794. https://doi.org/10.1177/14604086221079441

64 Donovan, N. (2022). Peer support facilitates post-traumatic growth in first responders: A literature review. *Trauma*, 24(4), 146040862210794. https://doi.org/10.1177/14604086221079441

65 Rollwage, M., Loosen, A., Hauser, T. U., Moran, R., Dolan, R. J., & Fleming, S. M. (2020). Confidence Drives a Neural Confirmation Bias. *Nature Communications*, 11(1). https://doi.org/10.1038/s41467-020-16278-6

66 Cleare, S., Gumley, A., & O'Connor, R. C. (2019). Self-compassion, Self-forgiveness, Suicidal ideation and Self-harm: a Systematic review. *Clinical Psychology & Psychotherapy*, 26(5). https://doi.org/10.1002/cpp.2372

67 Hermans, E. J., Hendler, T., & Kalisch, R. (2024). Building Resilience: The Stress Response as a Driving Force for Neuroplasticity and Adaptation. *Biological Psychiatry*, 97(4). https://doi.org/10.1016/j.biopsych.2024.10.016

68 *Purpose in Life Can Lead to Less Stress, Better Mental Well-being.* (2025). Psychiatry.org. https://www.psychiatry.org/news-room/apa-blogs/purpose-in-life-less-stress-better-mental-health?

69 Glass, O., Dreusicke, M., Evans, J., Bechard, E., & Wolever, R. Q. (2019). Expressive writing to improve resilience to trauma: A clinical feasibility trial. *Complementary Therapies in Clinical Practice*, 34(1), 240–246. https://doi.org/10.1016/j.ctcp.2018.12.005

70 Korhonen, M., Komulainen, K., & Okkonen, V. (2020). Burnout as an identity rupture in the life course: a longitudinal narrative method. *Sociology of Health & Illness*, 42(8), 1918–1933. https://doi.org/10.1111/1467-9566.13183

71 *Purpose in Life Can Lead to Less Stress, Better Mental Well-being.* (2025). Psychiatry.org. https://www.psychiatry.org/news-room/apa-blogs/purpose-in-life-less-stress-better-mental-health?

72 Korhonen, M., Komulainen, K., & Okkonen, V. (2020). Burnout as an identity rupture in the life course: a longitudinal narrative method. *Sociology of Health & Illness*, 42(8), 1918–1933. https://doi.org/10.1111/1467-9566.13183

73 Ozbay, F., Johnson, D. C., Dimoulas, E., Morgan, C., Charney, D., & Southwick, S. (2007). Social Support and Resilience to Stress: From Neurobiology to Clinical Practice. *Psychiatry (Edgmont)*, 4(5), 35–40. https://pmc.ncbi.nlm.nih.gov/articles/PMC2921311/

74   Lieberman, M. D., Eisenberger, N. I., Crockett, M. J., Tom, S. M., Pfeifer, J. H., & Way, B. M. (2007). Putting feelings into words: affect labeling disrupts amygdala activity in response to affective stimuli. *Psychological Science*, 18(5), 421–428. https://doi.org/10.1111/j.1467-9280.2007.01916.x

75   Korhonen, M., Komulainen, K., & Okkonen, V. (2020). Burnout as an identity rupture in the life course: a longitudinal narrative method. Sociology of Health & Illness, 42(8), 1918–1933.

76   Lieberman, M. D., Eisenberger, N. I., Crockett, M. J., Tom, S. M., Pfeifer, J. H., & Way, B. M. (2007). Putting feelings into words: affect labeling disrupts amygdala activity in response to affective stimuli. *Psychological Science*, 18(5), 421–428. https://doi.org/10.1111/j.1467-9280.2007.01916.x

77   Kramer, C. K., & Cristiane Bauermann Leitao. (2023). Laughter as medicine: A systematic review and meta-analysis of interventional studies evaluating the impact of spontaneous laughter on cortisol levels. *PLoS One*, 18(5), e0286260–e0286260. https://doi.org/10.1371/journal.pone.0286260

78   Rollwage, M., Loosen, A., Hauser, T. U., Moran, R., Dolan, R. J., & Fleming, S. M. (2020). Confidence Drives a Neural Confirmation Bias. *Nature Communications*, 11(1). https://doi.org/10.1038/s41467-020-16278-6

79   *Personality and Social Psychology Review* 1 -25. (n.d.). https://faculty.haas.berkeley.edu/jschroeder/Publications/Hobson%20et%20al%20Psychology%20of%20Rituals.pdf?

ACKNOWLEDGMENTS

To my husband and my boys, you are my heart, the bright moments when this work gets heavy. Thank you for your patience and your love when the mission pulled me thin. To my extended family, thank you for reminding me what I'm made of.

To my first responder family, the ones I've served beside, the ones I've coached, and the ones who've trusted me with your scars and your stories. Your grit, your honesty, and your willingness to keep showing up are the threads that hold this book together. Keep going. What you do matters more than you realize.

To the mentors and peers who supported me, challenged me, and encouraged me, your influence runs deeper than names on a page. The way you lead, the way you live, and the way you refuse to quit is proof that this fight is worth it.

To the crew who helped polish these pages, thank you for making sure the message was clear and strong.

And most importantly, to Jesus Christ, my Lord and Savior. Every shred of inspiration, every ounce of fortitude it took to write this, and every word here belongs to Him. All glory to God.

ABOUT THE AUTHOR

AK Dozanti, MA is a national keynote speaker, coach, and author of *Beat the Burnout: Prevention and Recovery Solutions for Frontline Professionals*, an Amazon #1 New Release in Law Enforcement. A wellness specialist and thought leader, she delivers the same clarity and directness first responders rely on in the field, blending grit, heart, and lived experience in a way that resonates deeply.

A former award-winning Deputy Sheriff and criminal court victim advocate, AK knows what it means to carry the weight of the job home and push through burnout when the world expects you to be unbreakable. Her own battle with burnout became the catalyst for Life Saver Wellness, where she now equips first responders with tools to regulate stress, expand capacity, and rise stronger without losing themselves in the process.

Her work has been featured in articles including in *Law Enforcement Today* and across dozens of podcasts. From national conferences to department training rooms, AK's voice continues to reach responders with hard truths and practical solutions that save and elevate the lives of the life savers.

For more information on AK Dozanti and Life Saver Wellness, visit akdozanti.com.

ALSO AVAILABLE

AK DOZANTI'S POWERFUL BOOK:

BEAT THE BURNOUT:
Prevention and Recovery Solutions for Frontline Burnout

Live Well. Serve Strong.

In high-stakes domains like frontline professions, we have to be intensely driven about what we do. Yet, sometimes, the demands and our passion burn so brightly that it leaves us feeling drained, agitated, and distracted. This book is a thoughtful guide designed to help you navigate the unique challenges faced by frontline work. Drawing from the teachings of experts, raw and real-life experiences, and extracting from your own wisdom, these chapters explore the complexities of burnout. Acknowledging that these issues cannot simply be resolved with a "suck it up" mentality, AK presents a path to healing, self-discovery, and excellence in homelife and career.

The steps on this path include:

- Recognizing mental and physical warning signs and contributing factors to burnout.

- Strategies for managing intense emotions that come with the job.

- Techniques for building strong relationships and social support networks.

- Practical advice for making self-care a priority

Practical tactics and actionable exercises, alongside remarkable research, will allow all first responders and frontline command staff to be empowered to recalibrate their lives and Beat the Burnout.

SOS

When it's bigger than a reset.
If you're in crisis, stop reading.
Scan the QR code below.

or dial 988 or 911

The QR Code above will take you to a list of trusted, responder-informed crisis resources, no ads, no BS, just help.

Use it if you're dealing with:

- Suicidal thoughts
- Panic attacks
- Flashbacks or dissociation
- Self-harm urges
- Substance use
- Anything that feels too heavy to handle alone

You don't need to figure it out first.

You just need to reach out.

Scan the code. Get support. Now.

LOCAL PEER SUPPORT PHONE NUMBERS:

_____

_____

_____

_____